METHUEN · ENGLISH · TEXTS
GENERAL EDITOR · JOHN DRAKAKIS

D0224763

JOHN CLARE
Selected Poetry and Prose

No man ever came so near to putting the life of the farm, as it is lived, not as it is seen over a gate, into poetry.

— Edward Thomas

There is no poet who in his nature poetry so completely subdues self and mood, and deals with the topic for its own sake.

— Edmund Blunden

Clare compensated for his restricted subject matter by looking more deeply and seeing much more clearly than the average person.

— M. and R. Williams, this vol.

He is the finest naturalist in all English poetry.

— Robinson and Summerfield

METHUEN · ENGLISH · TEXTS
GENERAL EDITOR · JOHN DRAKAKIS

JOHN CLARE

1793 - 1864 (in asylums from 1837 on)

Selected Poetry and Prose

Edited by
Merryn and Raymond Williams

For an appreciation of Clare, see:
Edward Thomas, A Literary Pilgrim,
p. 167-178.

METHUEN · LONDON AND NEW YORK

First published in 1986 by
Methuen & Co. Ltd
11 New Fetter Lane,
London EC4P 4EE

Published in the USA by
Methuen & Co.
in association with Methuen, Inc.
29 West 35th Street,
New York, NY 10001

Typeset in Great Britain by
Scarborough Typesetting Services
and printed by
Richard Clay, The Chaucer Press,
Bungay, Suffolk

British Library Cataloguing in Publication
Data

Clare, John, 1793–1864
Selected poetry and prose. – (Methuen
English texts)
I. Title   II. Williams, Merryn
III. Williams, Raymond, 1921–
828'.709   PR4453.C6

ISBN 0 416 41120 7

Library of Congress Cataloging in
Publication Data

Clare, John, 1793–1864.
John Clare: selected
(Methuen English texts)
Bibliography: p.
I. Williams, Merryn.   II. Williams,
Raymond.   III. Series.
PR4453.C6A6   1986
821'.7   86–12776

ISBN 0 416 41120 7 (pbk)

Contents

Published 1820 (handwritten, left margin)

Published 1821 (handwritten, left margin)

Published 1821

Introduction

Well in my many walks I rarely found
A place less likely for a bird to form
Its nest close by the rut gulled waggon road . . .

This voice, once heard, is unmistakable. Its public name is John Clare but beyond that hard-pressed and often uncertain identity it is a way of seeing and writing – often writing as speaking: 'well in my many walks' – which is a state of being, a condition of existence, long before and after it can be formally defined.

. . . And on the almost bare foot-trodden ground
With scarce a clump of grass to keep it warm
And not a thistle spreads its spears abroad
Or prickly bush to shield it from harms way
And yet so snugly made that none may spy
It out save accident – and you and I
Had surely passed it in our walk to day
Had chance not led us by it . . .

complete poem on p.139

The find is the nest of a pettichap; one of the warblers. As the poem continues the nest is intensely observed and described. Yet although the observation is precise and sustained it is the voice that stays with us: a rare but common voice.

It is more important for us to learn to listen to this voice – yet in a way it is not learning, it is often more like recognizing – than to

1

push past it to try to define the name and life we attach to it: John Clare. Yet we must also say, in justice, that this rare but common voice, in its long and troubled transactions with the available public world, struggled, at times desperately, to go beyond anonymity, to seal and stamp an acknowledged identity, an answering reputation. Thus we should try, with respect, to see the recorded life beyond the voice: the life that contained the voice. All we should not do is lead with the record, before the voice is listened to. For Clare, from the beginning, and in too many subsequent accounts, was seen from and through his public condition before what he was actually writing was heard as itself. The fact that he was a labourer; the fashionable label that he was a 'peasant poet'; the hard subsequent history of his confinement and death in an asylum: all belong to the record but cannot be permitted to muffle or, at worst, to override the voice.

To know what by shorthand we call Clare the voice is enough. To know more is to enter a much wider history, which is still not a real history unless this voice is part of it.

*

Can the facts of the life be simply recorded? It is technically possible, but every isolated and in that sense undoubted fact is, when properly seen, part of a wider and for the most part unvoiced history. With this reminder the simple record can be set down.

'There was five of us.' John was the elder of twins, born on 13 July 1793. His twin sister died in infancy. His mother, Ann Stimson, daughter of a shepherd, was then 36. She had been 35 when she married Parker Clare, then 32: son of the unmarried daughter of 'John Clare, <u>Clark</u>' and a Scottish fiddler and schoolmaster John Donald Parker. Parker Clare was a thresher, a wrestler and a singer of ballads and old songs. Ann Clare was illiterate. She contracted a painful dropsy some years after John's birth.

parish clerk

The place was Helpstone, in Northamptonshire: a village of some sixty families. The house was of stone, and thatched: a single house just then being divided in the general increase of population: now for the Clares two rooms down and two up, connected by a ladder; rent raised from 40 shillings to 3 guineas a year: eight or nine weeks' money in labouring wages.

[2] At age 13, his mind was temporarily unbalanced when he saw a neighbor break his neck by being thrown from a hay wage. At 16, he fell in love with Mary Joyce, daughter of a well-to-do farmer who forbade their meetings.

North and east of the village was the Peterborough Great Fen, then undrained and uncultivated. South and west were the Midland woods and fields and common-land heath.

Clare's childhood in this country belongs in his own voice. To summarize it is to lose it. But another history was beginning to make its way: dame school, to learn to read from the Bible and to write a little (then a common definition of elementary education); from 7 to 12 intermittent school at fourpence a week, while he earned twopence a week herding, bird-scaring or threshing with a child's small flail. Reading, writing, arithmetic; once a reward of sixpence for repeating aloud the third chapter of the Book of Job. Then from 12 to 16 night-school and day-labour: horse-ploughing and reaping; threshing; tending cattle. Talk of apprenticing to a shoemaker or a stonemason; 'shoyd off'. Application to be clerk at a lawyer's: rejected. Then at 16 a year's hire as farmboy to a publican; at 17 apprentice gardener at Burghley House; at 18 work for a nursery-man. In the next two to three years catchwork with labouring gangs, drilling with the militia being raised during the Napoleonic wars. From 20 to 23, back in Helpstone, day-labour, mainly gardening; spending much time in a neighbouring camp of gipsies. At 24 lime-burning in Rutland. A few miles north

But when he was 21 Clare had paid a week's wages for a manuscript book, to copy out some of the poems he had been writing since he was 13. He wrote on the title-page:

A Rustic's Pastime
in Leisure Hours
J. Clare
1814

He had bought the book from Henson, a printer and bookseller in Market Deeping, who was curious about its use. The long and tangled history of Clare's relations with booksellers and publishers followed from this contact. Through other printers and booksellers his growing body of poems made their way to a London publisher, John Taylor, who had already published Keats and Hazlitt. In 1820, under the title *Poems Descriptive of Rural Life and Scenery*, Clare's first

At 24, met his wife-to-be Patty Turner. Also issued a "proposal for publishing by subscription a collection of original verses." This was unsuccessful, and moreover Clare was fired from the limekiln for distributing his prospectus during working hours, forcing him to ask for parish relief.

3

collection was published. In the same year he married Patty (Martha) Turner.

*

Such accounts can be given and received within a familiar model of years of early hardship and the steady struggle for recognition and fame. It is not so much that the account is wrong; that exact movement is on the record. But it is also that the recognition, the fame, are not moments beyond time: abstract achievements in what can be generalized as a career. Clare's recognition and early success occurred within a model which was, so to say, waiting for him, and to which, from his whole situation, he had been preparing himself to adapt. There were difficulties even at first, as publishers and patrons offered their corrective advice. But the major difficulties came later, as the realities of this kind of recognition came through, and as the model itself disintegrated.

John Clare was not the first, but in effect the last, of the English 'peasant poets'. The label itself, and the cultural model it indicates, belongs to a historical period which was ending in Clare's early lifetime. The label tells us this, indirectly. *Peasant* had been used in English since the fifteenth century to describe people who worked as well as lived in the country, but by the eighteenth century it was a learned or literary word; the common native word was always *countryman*. Cobbett in 1830, with more indignation than accuracy, described *peasantry* as 'a *new* name given to the *country labourers* by the insolent boroughmongering and loan-mongering tribes'. It was not a new name but, after the major changes in English country life had reached their disintegrating climax in Cobbett's and in Clare's lifetimes, it was, if not always insolent, invariably external and in that sense indifferent to those to whom it appeared to point.

From an early period in these changes, *peasant* was in effect a cultural rather than a social description. The real economy of rural England, through the long period of enclosures and engrossings, had become a complex structure of landlords, tenants and landless labourers. Moreover, and just as important in its effects, the decisive economic structure of English society as a whole was coming to be based in mercantile capital and the money market. Peasants, in the

[4] "It is hard to imagine a combination with more possibilities for wretchedness than that of poet and agricultural labourer." — Edward Thomas

period of these changes, were now less those who worked on and inherited their little holdings of land – that class, indeed, was largely extinguished – than, from an external point of view, often specifically urban or metropolitan, an undifferentiated body of people to whom certain general qualities were ascribed. Cobbett picked up the insolent ascriptions: of roughness, rudeness, earthiness; the familiar descriptions as uneducated and ignorant. But the model would be very much simpler if it were only negative. In another external way of seeing, these same people were simple, honest and natural; blessed by a sweet and direct sensibility of all living things; virtuous and wise in their intimacy with nature. It was in the label of *peasant poet* that these two apparently incompatible ways of seeing country people were brought together in a single model.

Thus the peasant poet, it could be taken for granted, was *uneducated*, in a very deliberate and specializing sense. Strictly, since he (it was sometimes she) was writing poems in a period in which a majority of the whole population was still illiterate, the tag of *uneducated* might seem misplaced. At one level (as so often since, even in the quite different circumstances of universal education and literacy) the blank denial of any education meant in practice a persistent difficulty with changing levels of accuracy in the conventions of grammar and spelling. The writing was not enough; as 'uneducated' writing it had to be corrected in these respects. But at another level the lack of this formal correctness could be directly connected with the other half of the model: the freshness, the directness, the spontaneity of observation and feeling; the qualities that had supposedly been lost in the movement to a more *artificial* way of life and culture. Thus the poet was a peasant because his spelling and grammar were still uncertain, but the peasant was a poet because he had access to true and permanent natural experiences.

Any cultural model based on so deep a contradiction must eventually break down. Yet what such a model also shows is a need to bring together, to fuse (however improbably) contrary movements and values which are being historically experienced. The model of the peasant poet is part of a larger model, in which real discontinuities of condition and experience were mediated by forms of attempted continuity. The values of rural peace and content were never so widely celebrated as in this period of headlong change towards their opposites, and the celebration was not only by opponents of the changes but, significantly often, by their very promoters and associates. While a people was being remade, both voluntarily and forcibly, there was a conscious and popular revival of something believed to be older and deeper than this evident history: a recovery of the *folk*, of its songs and ballads, its beliefs and customs; a related transformation of the idea of *nature*, moving in one direction to its identification with human reason but in another direction to the sense of an inherent original power from which men and nations must humbly learn. Each aspect of this revival had its effect on ideas of the proper language of poetry, and these too supported and mediated, though still with contradictions, the idea of the peasant poet. Through him, it could be believed, both *the folk* and *nature* might speak.

The full development of this larger model did not end in Clare's lifetime. Indeed it is still, as we write, and even in some of its original forms, unfinished. But the specific instance of the peasant poet did end. It was not so much that it simply broke down. It could be said, with no exaggeration, that it blew up in Clare's face. For it is one thing to describe or anthologize these general movements of mind. It is quite another to live a practical life in the terms of a model which, whatever its general persuasiveness, has in reality to be not only a model but a livelihood.

How should a peasant poet live? While it is only a matter of the model, a simple condition can be prescribed. He should continue to be a poet, helped as necessary by patrons and friends, but he should also continue to be a peasant, since it is in that condition – and then only in that condition – that his value originates. But then the hard fact about the life of Clare – and it was not only his life, it was a common history – is that neither form of livelihood, as poet or peasant, was available on any reliable and continuing terms. The poet, whatever help he might get from patrons, was now in practice in the literary market; his livelihood and his next publication depended on copies sold. Meanwhile, as a peasant, in that increasingly artificial construction, there was no real livelihood either; its small independent propertied basis no longer reliably existed. The model might have been amended to the more accurate *labourer poet*: each man in this conjunction was dependent on selling his labour, if he could manage to be hired. But if we push the model to this more real description it breaks apart. The condition of selling one's labour, by hire, is not only a matter of this sale, that move, this fortunate or less fortunate circumstance. The idea of the peasant poet had a sense of property, of a certain kind, at its root: the property of being a peasant, the property of being a poet. Yet to go on being either, in these actual conditions, as labourer or writer or in any other form of hire, demanded recurrence, regularity, renewal: not one or a second opportunity, but repeated and reliable opportunities: the reasonable continuity that could indeed be assumed from property or establishment, but that in these changing times and conditions was not available anywhere in this class. So a man might be labourer or poet, as opportunity or need directed. To be both, and to go on being both, through ageing and sickness, was still a model but no longer either a livelihood or a life.

Stephen Duck from the 1730s; Mary Collier; Ann Yearsley; Henry Jones; Robert Bloomfield – through a century to John Clare this apparent lineage extends: the *peasant poets*, though their conditions and works are diverse and others even more unlike – Robert Tatersal, John Bryant – are, within the model, linked with them. There is still a sense in which we must emphasize the facts which the model offers to enclose. Both before and after their time there have been uncountable numbers of men and women who have found themselves classified, by the dominant social order and by the inequalities of income and education – also of gender – which such an order has imposed, as not belonging to that class of people from whom anything as deliberate as public writing should come. Indeed it is within that confident classification of exclusion that the culturally significant word *pretension* is formed. Yet whenever there have been even limited opportunities – though then always opportunities of a specific and shaping kind – it has been clear that there are gifted writers in this inevitably difficult situation: poets and historians, autobiographers and scholars, from social classes outside that class which has assumed or merely appropriated these practices and their direction to itself.

Public writing: but that is the core of the problem. It is not in the making of poems and songs and stories, or in the broadest sense in their publication, that the special difficulties of Clare and his fellows arise. It is in the specialization of such publication to printed works offered for sale. In other, mainly earlier, kinds of social order, different forms and relations were possible. Poets could be directly patronized by, even attached to, a settled rich household. Or they could be travelling performers, finding their livelihood from the communities they visited. Some of these forms survived the innovation and extension of print, but a literary market based on selling printed items steadily replaced them. By the time of Stephen Duck, and lasting through to the early years of Clare, even patronage was different in form: still sometimes in part a settled arrangement, a kind of pension guaranteeing a minimum livelihood – both Duck and Clare had this; but more generally a hybrid arrangement with the market: the subscription list of patrons, friends and well-wishers which guaranteed or promoted the first stage of market sale. By the end of Clare's writing life this hybrid in turn had virtually disappeared, and the full competitive market – at first without even the protection of copyright and royalties, in the new terms of literary property – was established. This market had differential effects: not only, as obviously, between commercially successful and unsuccessful writers – forms of success which by no means reliably corresponded with what was eventually reckoned to be literary merit – but also, and for Clare and others decisively, between forms of writing. In the fifteen years after Clare's first book of poems in 1820, there was a radical market shift away from verse and towards prose fiction. The novel, in serial and volume form, was the dominant literary form of the market by Clare's middle age. Poets, with only occasional exceptions, were from this time on pushed to the very edge of a market which yet, like many novelists, they wanted as a form of relationship with their readers, to disregard or supersede.

One special effect of this general situation has an interesting relevance to Clare. For the general social reasons already noticed, but also as a response to the new conditions of individual production for a competitive market, the idea of the *folk* as a cultural producer was becoming common. Necessarily this was inflected towards the past. Work that was probably of several different kinds – for by the nature of its survival its actual origins were and still often are uncertain – was brought together as a popular, in effect anonymous, tradition and was then contrasted with the new styles and conditions of production. Some of this work came from the old travelling performers; some from even earlier conditions of settlement or attachment in a rich and powerful household. Work of both kinds was also skilfully forged, to meet the new taste; other work was skilfully imitated, in a continuity of tradition; other works again were changed and developed, as commonly in an oral tradition.

John Clare was well placed to contribute to this tradition, if it had indeed still been a tradition rather than a revival which quickly took its place within the market. The only ancestors he could trace were 'Gardeners, Parish Clerks & fiddlers'. His father had a repertory of more than a hundred songs; John learned more from fiddling with the gipsies and himself collected 150 dances and folksong tunes. He seems also – the minutiae of the scholarship are difficult to interpret – to have written and rewritten many apparently traditional and new ballads.

Thus an older form of public composition was both within his hands and yet effectively powerless to help him. A certain kind of work, especially through the songs, was still marginally available, but the new dominance was of print. Moreover, in the period of Clare's youth and middle age, the printed forms through which these older kinds of composition and their contemporary successors were being distributed – in broadsides and in chapbook 'garlands' – were being effectively replaced by the new forms of popular print, in newspapers and magazines. The older forms did not all disappear, but the dominant tendency of the market went in this other direction. And it was again mainly fiction which was the beneficiary, especially in the magazines.

Thus Clare, in this as in other ways, was at a point of major cultural transition which he could not negotiate unaided. In his difficult circumstances, and under all the pressures which they put on his mind, he made his own way as a writer – the remarkable and continuing production is sufficient evidence of that – but to make his way through a lifetime as a public writer was, it now seems inevitably, beyond him.

published 1820, at age 27

publ. 1821

Clare's first book of poems sold 3000 copies in a year. His second book, *The Village Minstrel*, sold 1250. These are good figures, comparatively. Keats's *Lamia* had sold some 500. Wordsworth's *Excursion* reached 500 only in six years. To be sure Robert Bloomfield's *The Farmer's Boy* (1800) had sold 26,000 in three years (he still died in poverty), and Scott's *Marmion* had sold 11,000 in a year. In different forms, Cobbett's *Address to the Journeymen and Labourers* sold 200,000 and the *Last Dying Speech and Confession* of the murderer of Maria Marten a reputed 1,166,000. Yet, by the standards of the time, and for a first book of verse, the 3000 sales of *Poems Descriptive of Rural Life and Scenery* was a remarkable success, and Clare went to London to what seemed like triumph.

It is not easy to interpret the years immediately following. There were errors and broken promises, and beyond the difficult individual details the 1820s was in any case the decade in which the effects of a long cultural shift were becoming most apparent. There was a shift of literary fashions, there was intense political disturbance, and there was an upheaval in the financial conditions of publishing and bookselling. We can mark the change in Clare's case by the immediate public fortunes of *The Shepherd's Calendar*, published after delays in 1827 and selling only 425 copies.

It has to be emphasized that this change in public reception has no real relation to the quality of Clare's continuing work. On the contrary, it was as these difficulties closed in that, by the estimation of most later readers, Clare's best poems were being written. But the fashionable model of the peasant poet had gone. Clare wrote under increasing financial difficulties. Already in 1824 and 1825 he was speaking of his 'black melancholly' and of 'blue devils', and registering physical symptoms of 'numbness' and 'sinkings'; on one occasion he had an 'appoplectic fit'. In the same years he was sometimes writing under pseudonyms or ascribing his poems to other poets. In 1827 he attempted and abandoned a novel. He was

10 1820: Visited London, treated to acclaim, hailed as "The Northamptonshire Peasant Poet." Married Patty Turner shortly before the birth of their first child, on the strength of gifts from patrons (1820 or 21)

still doing field and gardening work, when he could get it, and especially earning at harvest. It has been estimated that in the last years of the decade, 1827 to 1830, he was getting some £50 a year: £40 from a fund established by patrons and publishers and subscribers, £10 from labouring and from occasional fees from periodicals. This income was well above the annual average for a labourer, but it was still a hard living, with a family and with his particular expenses for books, writing materials and postage. Moreover his health was troublesome: there was a serious illness in 1828, now variously and uncertainly described as the consequence of heavy drinking or some sexual disease; recovery from it was followed in 1830 by another serious illness and by evident mental problems, all difficult at this distance to diagnose reliably – modern estimates have varied from epileptiform attacks to schizophrenia and cyclothymic disorder. *by a patron*

In 1832, in an attempt to settle him, a move was made from Helpstone to a rented cottage with some land at Northborough. *Just three miles away from Helpstone* This was potentially an improvement in his material circumstances, but the effect of the move, on a man more deeply attached to his native Helpstone than others or perhaps even he at first understood, and already under major emotional pressures, was – in terms that now recover their literal meanings – unsettling, dislocating.

Yet he was still writing. Again he bought a large manuscript book and began preparing what he called *A Midsummer Cushion*, on the analogy of the gathering of wild flowers in a piece of turf which the people of his country took into their houses. It was a form of this collection that was published in 1835 as *The Rural Muse*: the change of title, and other corrections, indicate well enough the cultural distance between what Clare was actually writing and the models that with a patronizing kindness, were still being imposed on him. There is no Muse in these remarkably direct and observing, metrically skilful poems, but it is what he said on another occasion:

we have a many woods on one hand and a many nightingales, but no Chloes or Phillises worth the mention.

For this was not pastoral poetry: this was country poetry. The long

11

tension between the two kinds had reached breaking-point. Yet, as *The Rural Muse*, the collection sold reasonably well.

Clare's life, however, was beginning to break up. His mother died in 1835 and his father came to live with John and Patty and their seven children. Clare's own mental condition was now very disturbed, and there was talk of an asylum. From 1836 there are records of what was to prove a persistent delusion about Mary Joyce, a girl whom he had met as a schoolfriend aged 12 and seen often and wanted to marry when he was 16 and 17. She was living (until 1838), unmarried, only three miles away, but Clare now often believed that he had married her and that Patty, whom he loved, was his second wife.

In the summer of 1837, at the age of 44, Clare entered an asylum near Epping as a voluntary patient. He was to stay there until he escaped and walked home in 1841. His physician, Dr Allen, recorded in 1840: *on the northern outskirts of London*

> He has never been able to maintain in conversation, nor even in writing prose, the appearance of sanity for two minutes or two lines together, and yet there is no indication whatever of insanity in any of his poetry.

He was back in Northborough for only five months. He was then removed to the Northampton County Asylum, where he was kept until he died at the age of 70, in May 1864. Intermittently, while he was in the asylum, he continued to write poems and letters. An important group of poems was written between 1844 and 1850, and there were others, though increasingly infrequent, until the winter before his death. The poems contrast remarkably with several of his letters from the asylum, which are often lost in delusion, and with reports of his condition by visitors. He often told visitors that he was a prizefighter, and in 1845 is reported to have said: 'Oh poetry, ah, I know, I once had something to do with poetry, a long time ago, but it was no good. I wish, though, they could get a man with courage enough to fight me.' In 1860 he is reported to have said: 'Literature has destroyed my head and brought me here.' Yet at other times he saw the asylum as imprisonment: 'I am in Prison because I wont leave my family and tell a falshood.'

12   *While at Northampton Asylum, he was often allowed to go sit under the portico of a nearby church, where he could watch the gambols of children around him,*

*

The model of the *peasant poet*, as a way of enclosing Clare, has now lapsed. In its place, however, is a new yet obliquely related model: the *poet as rural victim*. Clare, for all his singularity, is still commonly enrolled in that version of the loss of an organic rural society which is typically summarized in a single word: *enclosure*.

It is worth pausing, before we look at the actual social changes which Clare experienced and in his own way interpreted, to ask how far such a description as *victim* can really be applied to him. To question the description is not to overlook or underrate the times of great suffering in his life. But, even at the simplest level, we do have to notice that he survived the phases of physical illness and lived to a sound 70 years. Moreover, through all the phases of physical and mental illness he went on doing what was always most important to him: writing his poems. By any ordinary comparative standard he was a remarkably productive poet, for all the difficult and changing circumstances of his life. This achievement ought not to be reduced to a label of *victim*. Against all the odds Clare made his way, in his most essential activity, however much he and others might see his life as a failure. Indeed, it is not quite impossible to see some of the most difficult shifts and passages in his life as specific, if unconscious yet usually successful, ways of going on writing poems against other pressures and claims. What can we make, for example, of that bewildered sadness: 'I once had something to do with poetry, a long time ago, but it was no good', in a period in which he was still actually writing some of his most interesting poems?

However this may be, the distance of his actual achievement from anything like the status of a victim is too great to be overlooked. A deep sympathy with Clare is inevitable, and the sadness can be overwhelming even when it is, as it must be, set beside the equally evident joy and energy. But there are too many real victims of that cruel time – men, women and children whose lives really were repressed, deformed, starved, extinguished – to allow any loose assimilation of this quite different, dislocated but remarkably persistent figure. Through all the neglect and the suffering, Clare's work is a special kind of triumph: a strong, unforgettable voice where so many millions in his condition were, as history now accounts them, voiceless.

This point bears especially on our understanding of the changes in rural society. There are complicated historical arguments about the actual effects of enclosure, including its specific effects in Helpstone. Modern capitalist accounts stress its undoubted contribution to increased agricultural productivity, and with others relate this to that rapid increase in population which was more often an immediate cause of dislocation and distress. Against these accounts we have to set a wider history, not limited to the period of parliamentary enclosures, in which a new social structure, in new relations between social classes, was establishing itself in England. There is reality in the accounts of many movements from small independence to pauperization: many marginal livelihoods were indeed extinguished. But in its most common form the summary of the major changes in the single term 'enclosure' is misleading, not least because it implies, always misleadingly and sometimes grossly, a happy and natural rural society before these particular changes.

Nothing in the long record allows us to believe this. There was no fall from an Eden, but rather a new phase of the long conquest and repression of working country people by wave after wave of land-lords and masters. Within this long history there were temporary settlements, improvements, accommodations, as chance and opportunity and phases of the general economy allowed. But the broad tendency of conquest and appropriation, using every kind of legal and illegal means, had begun long before any time to which Clare could trace his ancestors and was to continue, in new ways, long after him.

Yet the very opening out of this new social order had paradoxical effects. The capitalist rural economy involved new kinds of exploitation, but by its very nature opened up new kinds of mobility and cultural contact. This paradox is precisely relevant to Clare. The dislocation of his contacts with print and poetry is even more important, in his life, than the shifts and dislocations in working conditions on the land. He regularly and accurately saw himself as a poor man, and as such bitterly resented the tyranny – it is his repeated word – of local and more distant masters. But his exposure

14 Even ecologically, there is something to be said for enclosure. The hedges and stone walls resulting from enclosure provided valuable wildlife habitat. Environmentalists nowadays protest the clearing of these uncultivated borders.

to them, in his requirement to be hired – a requirement which his father had shared, with millions of others, before enclosure – was shot through with his consciousness that he knew of and wanted to do quite another kind of work. The convincing complaints, especially in the early poems, of the tyranny and indifference of the masters are almost inextricably intertwined with complaints about the indifference or worse of his neighbours to the new kind of work – the writing – which had come to mean everything to him.

Enclosure, then, in Clare's verse, is a complex and shifting term. It is the cry of his class and generation against their fundamental subordination, concentrated in an outcry against the most immediate and most visible phase of change. As such he runs it through a variety of themes, from the explicitly social and political to the explicitly natural and local. The closure of commons, the stopping of paths; loss of labour and of wages; the ploughing of meadows and the felling of trees: all these, on different occasions, and often effectively and rhetorically combined, are the felt consequences of what is at once the 'mildew' and the 'tyranny' of enclosure.

His political attitudes are part of the same range. He knew himself to be poor and saw the poor man as 'an alien in a strange land'. He believed, with the radicals of his day, that 'the prosperity of one class was founded on the adversity and distress of the other'. He also distrusted what he knew as politics, in ways that have been misunderstood by commentators writing from the quite different political world of universal suffrage. Politics, as he knew it, as a matter from which he and his class were deliberately excluded, was 'an art of money catching', 'a game of hide-&-seek for self interest . . . the terms wig and tory are nothing more in my mind than the left and right hand of that monster'. Under early pressure from his patrons to 'expunge, expunge' such words as 'accursed Wealth' from his 'child-of-nature' verses, and within his often withdrawing and evading cast of mind, he distanced himself deliberately from militant radicalism; he wanted, he said, 'a reform that would do good and hurt none', and this in, of all years, 1830, when much of rural England was in revolt.

There is then a further complication within the paradox mentioned above. He wanted a greatly increased popular education;

he had known the need for it. But this was in terms of his own problems of affiliation and of his early and persistent attitudes to his fellow-labourers and neighbours: 'the dull and obstinate class from whence I struggled into light'. That bitter and alienating observation, so often repeated by men in comparable conditions and with comparable vocations and gifts, rang through what he could nevertheless continue to see as general oppression and cruel indifference.

The early poems, written in an available tradition of rural distress and retrospective lament and powerfully reinforcing it, often contain this specific and distancing complaint:

> Bred in a village full of strife and noise,
> Old senseless gossips, and blackguarding boys,
> Ploughmen and threshers, whose discourses led
> To nothing more than labour's rude employs . . .

This is the complication: a class consciousness which is most sharply experienced as an alienated individual consciousness; the knowledge of a spectrum of deprivation which, as he directly experiences it, really does run from the more readily acknowledged and recorded facts of low wages and high prices, the humiliations of hirings, to the more painful and sometimes more immediate recognition of limited knowledge, limited interests, limited tolerance of other possible ways.

This complex is then interpreted, in an intensely personal way, as a double deprivation: at once poverty and a cultural block. It is also, in its outcome, a specific alienation: an alienation which he sought to overcome in the literary market, which then in turn alienated him. That succession of problems is what can be seen as making Clare a victim. But in fact, remarkably, he found a way of negotiating it in his developing verse. He attached himself to what was still, through all the changes, present: the specific and diverse physical world of his own place – the trees, the birds, the flowers, the weather: the mid-summer cushion which he could make in his own way. He was still to write in other moods and forms, in a remarkably wide range. But it was here that he became the kind of writer who connects most readily with a widespread modern form of consciousness. What had been complained of, among others by Keats, in the early poems – that 'description too much prevailed over the sentiment', that he was not, as was expected, attaching natural objects to ideas or to received cultural forms – was to become more emphatic and more deliberate. He had answered back to Keats:

> His descriptions of scenery are often very fine but as it is the case with other inhabitants of great citys he often described nature as she appeared to his fancys & not as he would have described her had he witnessed the things he describes . . . what appear as beautys in the eyes of a pent up citizen are looked upon as conceits by those who live in the country.

This is not only the rejection of natural-philosophical and pastoral poetry, it is the announcement of an insistence on direct observation. An observation, moreover, which is also a direct participation: that of the inhabitant, the self-locator, who shares with the natural world what he cannot share either with the pressing and destructive social order or with his own class and labour. It is a very significant moment of change in English poetry: a particular arrival, through deep social alienation, at a lively natural participation.

*

This is why we cannot usefully see Clare as a victim. His central work is a change in sensibility, involving both losses and gains, which readily connects with strains and developments in our own still altering world. The directly social and political responses go into another, increasingly active tradition. The older poetry, which had enclosed natural observation within classical and other ideological models, also went on, but now – with the contrasting example of Clare and others – in more obviously distanced and questionable ways. Clare put a specific new voice into English writing, and it was a voice of his class though not through his class. An intensely physical sensibility found its natural writing forms.

Clare was always a conscious craftsman: both in seeking models in other poets, whom he could often skilfully imitate or consciously absorb, and in that practical sense of the intent selection of words and rhythms which he learned not only from his literary models but from

"An insistence on direct observation" is the 17
positive side. Edward Thomas notes the
negative side "[His poetry] was only thinly
tinged with his personality."

the orally transmitted songs and ballads which he had looked for a notation to record. This craft was always more than the simplicities of 'nature's child'; it was a conscious apprenticeship in a studied world:

> From Donns old homely gold whose broken feet
> Jostles the reader's patience from its seat
> To Popes smooth rhymes that regularly play
> In musics stated periods all the way
> That starts and closes starts again and times
> Its tuning gammut true as minster chimes
> From these old fashions stranger metres flow
> Half prose half verse that stagger as they go
> One line starts smooth and then for room perplext
> Elbows along and knocks against the next
> And half its neighbour where a pause marks time
> There the clause ends what follows is for ryhme

Clare's neglect of punctuation deprives us of a familiar pointing: one of the elements of the shaping of print. Often we have to remember what he called the 'breathing word': sometimes, as in 'The pettichaps nest', the voice moving in the run of talk with a friend; at other times, as in 'Mary', with the tune of a song very close to it, shaping it for a page. He attempts and controls so many of these diverse rhythms, as well as those of Thomson, Goldsmith and Gray, Cowper, Crabbe and Byron, which he directly absorbed and reproduced, that there can be no accurate reduction to a single strain. Yet in almost all of them there is a particular, recognizable Clare voice: a breathing, a naming, an intense physical presence.

This, then, is the paradox of his life and work: an intensely persistent, indeed unbreakable sensibility, which finds a remarkable diversity in his poetic forms and yet, in the life, breaks into that radical uncertainty of identity which in its everyday passages became a form of madness. In his later years he knew this condition directly: 'I am – yet what I am, none cares or knows.' In that strain there is an available reading of simple neglect by others, an isolation coming from others; and this is indeed strongly and repeatedly felt. But there is always more to it than that. The sense of strangeness, a feeling of failure to recognize and relate to others, is also part of the condition:

> Even the dearest, that I love the best
> Are strange – nay, rather stranger than the rest.

And finally there is the real break, the effectively total alienation:

> I feel I am; – I only know I am
> And plod upon the earth, as dull and void.

What is most difficult to understand, beyond the simple labels of success and failure, sanity and madness, is the persistence of an active, creative sensibility – in that sense an identity which across the years we can instantly recognize – within a disintegration of virtually all the available identities, identifications, of a person in an actual time. During his first years in the Northampton asylum he claimed that he had been an eye witness of the execution of Charles I and of the Battle of the Nile. The creative reconstruction, which he seems to have managed with the skill and the memory of the oral and printed tales of his boyhood, had broken loose from where it would be recognized, as public writing, and become private madness. He could sometimes hang on, especially in his verse, to his identity as poet, but he would also repeatedly claim to be different named prizefighters and military heroes. In his letters, though known names and relationships are often acknowledged, there is not only the persistent delusion of the marriage to Mary Joyce but also radical confusion of names and relationships and generations.

Or there is, finally, this: pathetically reported. Talking with a visitor, he had quoted well-known lines by Shakespeare and by Byron as his own. When the visitor objected he replied: 'I'm John Clare now. I was Byron and Shakespeare formerly. At different times you know I'm different people – that is the same person with different names.' At an everyday level this is simple madness, of a familiar kind, even when we have allowed, as sometimes we must, for an element of self-protective play, a certain quickness of habitual evasion. There are other times when no borderline needs to be crossed, though this or that visitor saw him beyond it. When he said, in a conversation, 'I know Gray', it is not necessarily the delusion of being out of his time, knowing a poet who had died before he was born, as which it was taken; it is, at one recognizable level of the mind, a genuine and acceptable connection; this is where, with another poet, he belonged and felt himself only to belong.

But 'at different times you know I'm different people'? This is the reality of alienation. What it brought was suffering, not only to himself but to all those near to him: his specific rejections were as painful as his own sense of rejection. What remains as extraordinary is what Dr Allen had noted: 'there is no indication whatever of insanity in any of his poetry': a judgement which for all the difficulty of the terms we can still for all practical purposes endorse. What survived, within an otherwise broken mind, was the process which had always been central, what everything had been sacrificed for. It would be easy, at this distance, to idealize it, but it is too hard and painful for that. What we can say, though, is that it makes sense of a kind – sense for him in the persistence of the sound and process of verse itself – to say 'I was Byron and Shakespeare formerly'. The act and continuity of composing had broken loose from its settlement in a social identity and in historical time. But the physical being stubbornly persisted and, within that being, and not only in the verse, there was still a particular physical world: birds, flowers, brooks, rain, the seasons:

And every place the Poet trod
And every place the Poet sung.

*

The record, and the attempt to understand it, need to be made. Clare requires what he asked for in his life: the continuity of an acknowledged identity; an answering reputation. Yet though it can be properly offered, in record and interpretation, assurance can come only in his own voice: in these and others of his writings.

A NOTE ON THE TEXT

Earlier editions of Clare differ considerably from the more modern ones. His first publishers corrected his spelling, tidied up his grammar, and often left out several sections of a poem. We have tried to present the poetry and prose exactly as Clare wrote it. Except for the items listed below, the text followed is *The Oxford Authors: John Clare* (Oxford, 1984), edited by Eric Robinson and David Powell.

'I was born at Helpstone', 'Grammar'   From *Sketches in the Life of John Clare* (London, 1931), edited by Edmund Blunden.

'The village minstrel', 'England, 1830', 'Schoolboys in winter', 'The foddering boy'   The text used here is *The Poems of John Clare* (London, 1935), edited with an introduction by J. W. Tibble.

'A Sunday with shepherds and herdboys', 'The ragwort'   From *Selected Poems and Prose of John Clare* (Oxford, 1967), edited by Eric Robinson and Geoffrey Summerfield.

'The parish'   From *The Parish* (Harmondsworth, 1985), edited by Eric Robinson.

'The flood'   The first and third verses were printed in *The Rural Muse* (1835) as if they were separate sonnets. The second verse appeared in Tibble's 1935 edition (op. cit.) for the first time. It should be read as a single poem.

'London versus Epping Forest'   From *Later Poems of John Clare 1837–64* (Oxford, 1984), edited by Eric Robinson and David Powell.

'Byron's funeral'   The text used here appears in the notes to *The Life of John Clare* (1865) by Frederick W. Martin, edited with an introduction and notes by Eric Robinson and Geoffrey Summerfield (London, 1964).

The editors and publishers would like to thank the copyright holders for permission to reproduce the following items:

'My first attempts at poetry', 'Going for a soldier', 'A prophet is nothing in his own country', 'The autobiography', 'Memories of childhood', 'Snakes', 'Byron's funeral', 'Letter to James Hipkins'   From *The Prose of John Clare* (London, 1951), edited by J. W. and Anne Tibble.

'The green woodpecker's nest', 'Woodpecker's nest', 'The puddock's nest' From *Bird's Nest, Poems by John Clare* (Ashington, Northumberland, 1973), edited by Anne Tibble, reproduced by permission of Mid Northumberland Arts Group.

'Don Juan A poem', 'Child Harold', 'Lord hear my prayer when trouble glooms', 'Song', 'There is a charm in solitude that cheers', 'Fragment' From *Poems of John Clare's Madness* (London, 1949), edited by Geoffrey Grigson. ('Child Harold' was not published as a complete poem until 1949, but parts of it appear in separate poems: 'The exile', 'The return: Northborough, 1841', and 'September mornings', in Tibble (1935), op. cit.)

'Song last day', 'Look through the naked bramble and black thorn' From *The Shepherd's Calendar* (Oxford, 1964), edited by Eric Robinson and Geoffrey Summerfield. Copyright Eric Robinson. Reproduced by permission of Curtis Brown Ltd.

NB Square brackets enclosing text indicate words or lines published in the first edition of Clare's work in 1820 but not present in the manuscripts. An ellipsis in square brackets in an extract indicates where we have omitted text.

JOHN CLARE
Selected Poetry and Prose

HELPSTONE

Hail humble Helpstone where thy valies spread
And thy mean village lifts its lowly head
Unknown to grandeur and unknown to fame
No minstrel boasting to advance thy name
Unletterd spot unheard in poets' song
Where bustling labour drives the hours along
Where dawning genius never met the day
Where useless ign'rance slumbers life away
Unknown nor heeded where low genius trys
Above the vulgar and the vain to rise   10
Whose low opinions rising thoughts subdue
Whose railing envy damps each humble view
Oh where can friendships cheering smiles abode
To guide young wanderers on a doubtful road
The trembling hand to lead, the steps to guide
And each vain wish (as reason proves) to chide –
Mysterious fate who can on thee depend
Thou opes the hour but hides its doubtful end
In fancys view the joys have long appear'd
Where the glad heart by laughing plenty's cheer'd   20
And fancys eyes as oft as vainly fill
At first but doubtful and as doubtful still

So little birds in winters frost and snow
Doom'd (like to me) wants keener frost to know
Searching for food and 'better life' in vain
(Each hopeful track the yielding snows retain)
First on the ground each fairy dream pursue
Tho sought in vain – yet bent on higher view
Still chirp and hope and wipe each glossy bill
Nor undiscourag'd nor disheartn'd still   30
Hop on the snow cloth'd bough and chirp again
Heedless of naked shade and frozen plain
With fruitless hopes each little bosom warms
Springs budding promise – summers plentious charms

---

* Numbers in square brackets refer to pages on which notes may be found

A universal hope the whole prevades
And chirping plaudits fill the chilling shades
Till warm'd at once the vain deluded flies
And twitatwit their visions as they rise
Visions like mine that vanish as they flye
In each keen blast that fills the higher skye   40
Who find like me along their weary way
Each prospect lessen and each hope decay
And like to me these victims of the blast
(Each foolish fruitless wish resign'd at last)
Are glad to seek the place from whence they went
And put up with distress and be content –

Hail scenes obscure so near and dear to me
The church the brook the cottage and the tree
Still shall obscurity rehearse the song
And hum your beauties as I stroll along   50
Dear native spot which length of time endears
The sweet retreat of twenty lingering years
And oh those years of infancy the scene
Those dear delights where once they all have been
Those golden days long vanish'd from the plain
Those sports those pastimes now belovd in vain
When happy youth in pleasures circle ran
Nor thought what pains awaited future man
No other thought employing or employ'd
But how to add to happiness enjoy'd   60
Each morning wak'd with hopes before unknown
And eve possesing made each wish their own
The day gone bye left no pursuit undone
Nor one vain wish save that they went too soon
Each sport each pastime ready at their call
As soon as wanted they posses'd em all
These joys all known in happy infancy
And all I ever knew were spent on thee
And who but loves to view where these were past
And who that views but loves them to the last   70

26

Feels his heart warm to view his native place
A fondness still those past delights to trace
The vanish'd green to mourn the spot to see
Where flourish'd many a bush and many a tree
Where once the brook for now the brook is gone
Oer pebbles dimpling sweet went whimpering on
Oft on whose oaken plank I've wondering stood
(That led a pathway o'er its gentle flood)
To see the beetles their wild mazes run
With jetty jackets glittering in the sun   80
So apt and ready at their reels they seem
So true the dance is figur'd on the stream
Such justness such correctness they impart
They seem as ready as if taught by art
In those past days for then I lov'd the shade
How oft I've sighd at alterations made
To see the woodmans cruel axe employ'd
A tree beheaded or a bush destroy'd
Nay e'en a post old standard or a stone
Moss'd o'er by age and branded as her own   90
Would in my mind a strong attachment gain
A fond desire that there they might remain
And all old favourites fond taste approves
Griev'd me at heart to witness their removes

Thou far fled pasture long evanish'd scene
Where nature's freedom spread the flowry green
Where golden kingcups open'd in to view
Where silver dazies charm'd the 'raptur'd view
And tottering hid amidst those brighter gems
Where silver grasses bent their tiny stems   100
Where the pale lilac mean and lowly grew
Courting in vain each gazer's heedless view
While cowslaps sweetest flowers upon the plain
Seemingly bow'd to shun the hand in vain
Where lowing oxen roamd to feed at large
And bleating there the shepherd's woolly charge

Whose constant calls thy echoing vallies cheer'd
Thy scenes adornd and rural life endeard
No calls of hunger Pity's feelings wound
Twas wanton Plenty rais'd the joyful sound   110
Thy grass in plenty gave the wish'd supply
Ere sultry suns had wak'd the troubling fly
Then blest retiring by thy bounty fed
They sought thy shades and found an easy bed

But now alas those scenes exist no more
The pride of life with thee (like mine) is oer
Thy pleasing spots to which fond memory clings
Sweet cooling shades and soft refreshing springs
And though fate's pleas'd to lay their beauties by
In a dark corner of obscurity   120
As fair and sweet they bloom'd thy plains among
As blooms those Edens by the poets sung
Now all laid waste by desolations hand
Whose cursed weapon levels half the land
Oh who could see my dear green willows fall
What feeling heart but dropt a tear for all
Accursed wealth o'er bounding human laws
Of every evil thou remainst the cause
Victims of want those wretches such as me
Too truly lay their wretchedness to thee   130
Thou art the bar that keeps from being fed
And thine our loss of labour and of bread
Thou art the cause that levels every tree
And woods bow down to clear a way for thee

Sweet rest and peace ye dear departed charms
Which once industry cherish'd in her arms
When Peace and Plenty known but now to few
Were known to all and labour had his due
When mirth and toil companions thro' the day
Made labour light and pass'd the hours away   140

28

When nature made the fields so dear to me
Thin scattering many a bush and many a tree
Where the wood minstrels sweetly join'd among
And cheer'd my needy toilings with a song

Ye perishd spots adieu ye ruin'd scenes
Ye well-known pastures oft frequented greens
Though now no more – fond memory's pleasing pains
Within her breast your every scene retains
Scarce did a bush spread its romantic bower
To shield the lazy shepherd from the shower   150
Scarce did a tree befriend the chattering pye
By lifting up its head so proud and high
(Whose nest stuck on the topmost bough sublime
Mocking the efforts of each boy to climb
Oft as they've fill'd my vain desiring eye
As oft in vain my skill essay'd to try)
Nor bush nor tree within thy vallies grew
When a mischevious boy but what I knew
No not a secret spot did then remain
Through out each spreading wood and winding plain   160
But in those days my presence once possest
The snail horn searching or the mossy nest

Oh happy Eden of those golden years
Which mem'ry cherishes and use endears
Thou dear beloved spot may it be thine
To add a comfort to my life's decline
When this vain world and I have nearly done
And Time's drain'd glass has little left to run
When all the hopes that charm'd me once are oer
To warm my soul in extacy no more   170
By dissapointments prov'd a foolish cheat
Each ending bitter and beginning sweet
When weary age the grave a rescue seeks
And prints its image on my wrinkl'd cheeks
Those charms of youth that I again may see

29

May it be mine to meet my end in thee
And as reward for all my troubles past
Find one hope true to die at home at last

So when the traveller uncertain roams
On lost roads leading every where but home   180
Each vain desire that leaves his heart in pain
Each fruitless hope to cherish it in vain
Each hated track so slowly left behind
Makes for the home which night denies to find
And every wish that leaves the aching breast
Flies to the spot where all its wishes rest

Composed 1809–13   *First published 1820*

'I WAS BORN AT HELPSTONE'

I was born July 13, 1793, at Helpstone, a gloomy village in
Northamptonshire, on the brink of the Lincolnshire fens; my
mother's maiden name was Stimson, a native of Caistor, a
neighboring village, whose father was a town shepherd as they
are called, who has the care of all the flocks of the village; my
father was one of fate's chancelings, who drop into the world
without the honour of matrimony. He took the surname of his
mother, who to commemorate the memory of a worthless
father with more tenderness of lovelorn feeling than he
doubtless deserv'd, gave him his surname at his christening,   10
who was a Scotchman by birth, and a schoolmaster by profes-
sion, and in this stay at this, and the neighboring villages,
went by the name of John Donald Parker. This I had from John
Cue of Ufford, an old man who in his young days was a companion and confidential to my run-a-gate of a grandfather; for
he left the village and my grandmother, soon after the deplor-
able accident of misplaced love was revealed to him; but her
love was not that frenzy which shortens the days of the victim

of seduction, for she liv'd to the age of 86, and left this world
of troubles, Jan. 1, 1820.

Both my parents was illiterate to the last degree, my mother
knew not a single letter, and superstition went so far with her
that she believed the higher parts of learning was the blackest
arts of witchcraft, and that no other means could attain them;
my father could read a little in a Bible, or testament, and was
very fond of the superstitious tales that are hawked about a
street for a penny, such as old Nixon's Prophesies, Mother
Bunches Fairy Tales, and Mother Shipton's Legacy, &c., &c.;
he was likewise fond of Ballads, and I have heard him make a
boast of it over his horn of ale, with his merry companions,
that he coud sing or recite above a hundred; he had a tolerable
good voice, and was often called upon to sing at those con-
vivials of bacchanalian merry makings.

In my early years I was of a waukly constitution, so much
so, that my mother often told me she never could have dreamt
I should live to make a man, while the sister that was born
with me, being a twin, was as much to the contrary, a fine
lively bonny wench, whose turn it was to die first; she lived
but a few weeks, proving the old saying for once mistaken,
'that the weakest always goeth to the wall.' As my parents had
the good fate to have but a small family, I being the eldest of 4,
two of whom dyed in their Infancy, my mother's hopeful
ambition ran high of being able to make me a good scholar, as
she said she experienced enough in her own case to avoid
bringing up her children in ignorance; but God help her, her
hopeful and tender kindness was often cross'd with difficulty,
for there was often enough to do to keep cart upon wheels, as
the saying is, without incurring an extra expence of pulling me
to school, though she never lost the opportunity when she was
able to send me, nor woud my father interfere till downright
necessity from poverty forced him to check her kind
intentions; for he was a tender father to his children, and I have
every reason to turn to their memories with the warmest feelings of gratitude, and satisfaction; and if doing well to their
children be an addition to rightousness, I am certain, God

cannot forget to bless them with a portion of felicity in the other world, when souls are called to judgment, and receive the reward due to their actions committed below.

In cases of extreme poverty, my father took me to labour with him, and made me a light flail for threshing, learning me betimes the hardship which Adam and Eve inflicted on their children by their inexperienced misdeeds, incurring the perpetual curse from God of labouring for a livelihood, which the teeming earth is said to have produced of itself before. But use is second nature, at least it learns us patience; I resigned myself willingly to the hardest toils, and tho' one of the weakest, was stubborn and stomachful, and never flinched from the roughest labour; by that means, I always secured the favour of my masters, and escaped the ignominy that brands the name of idleness; my character was always 'weak but willing.' I believe I was not older than 10 when my father took me to seek the scanty rewards of industry; Winter was generally my season of imprisonment in the dusty barn, Spring and Summer my assistance was wanted elsewhere, in tending sheep or horses in the fields, or scaring birds from the grain, or weeding it; which was a delightful employment, as the old women's memories never failed of tales to smoothen our labour; for as every day came, new Giants, Hobgoblins, and fairies was ready to pass it away.

As to my schooling, I think never a year pass'd me till I was 11, or 12, but 3 months or more at the worst of times was luckily spared for my improvement, first with an old woman in the village, and latterly with a master at a distance from it. Here soon as I began to learn to write, the readiness of the Boys always practising urged and prompted my ambition to make the best use of my absence from school, as well as at it, and my master was always surprised to find me improved every fresh visit, instead of having lost what I had learned before; for which, to my benefit, he never failed to give me tokens of encouragement. Never a leisure hour pass'd me without making use of it; every winter night, our once unlettered hut was wonderfully changed in its appearance to a schoolroom.

The old table, which, old as it was, doubtless never was honoured with higher employment all its days then the convenience of bearing at meal times the luxury of a barley loaf, or dish of potatoes, was now covered with the rude beggings of scientifical requisitions, pens, ink, and paper, – one hour, hobbling the pen at sheephooks and tarbottles, and another, trying on a slate a knotty question in Numeration, or Pounds, Shillings and Pence; at which times my parents' triumphant   100
anxiety was pleasingly experienced; for my mother woud often stop her wheel, or look off from her work, to urge with a smile of the warmest rapture in my father's face her prophesy of my success, saying 'she'd be bound I shoud one day be able to reward them with my pen for the trouble they had taken in giving me schooling.'

And I have to return hearty thanks to a kind providence in bringing her prophesy to pass, and giving me the pleasure of being able to stay the storm of poverty and smoothen their latter days, and as a recompense for the rough beginnings of life,   110
bid their tottering steps decline in peaceful tranquillity to their long home, the grave. Here my highest ambition was gratify'd, for my greatest wish was to let my parents see a printed copy of my poems; that pleasure I have witness'd [. . .]

Composed 1821   First published 1931

NOON

All how silent and how still,
Nothing heard but yonder mill;
While the dazzled eye surveys
All around a liquid blaze;
And amid the scorching gleams,
If we earnest look it seems
As if crooked bits of glass
Seem'd repeatedly to pass.
O! for a puffing breeze to blow,
But breezes all are strangers now.   10

Not a twig is seen to shake,
Nor the smallest bent to quake;   *grass stem*
From the river's muddy side,
Not a curve is seen to glide;
And no longer on the stream,
Watching lies the silver bream,
Forcing from repeated springs,
'Verges in successive rings'.
Bees are faint and cease to hum,
Birds are overpow'r'd and dumb;   20
And no more love's oaten strains,   *oat stems used as musical*
Sweetly through the air complains;   *pipes*
Rural voices all are mute;
Tuneless lies the pipe and flute;
Shepherds with their panting sheep,
In the swaliest corner creep;
And from the tormenting heat,
All are wishing to retreat;
Huddled up in grass and flow'rs,
Mowers wait for cooler hours;   30
And the cow-boy seeks the sedge,
Ramping in the woodland hedge,
While his cattle o'er the vales,
Scamper with uplifted tails;
Others not so wild and mad,
That can better bear the gad,   *biting fly*
Underneath the hedge-row lunge,
Or, if nigh, in waters plunge;
O to see how flow'rs are took!
How it grieves me when I look: –   40
Ragged-robbins once so pink
Now are turn'd as black as ink,
And their leaves being scorch'd so much
Even crumble at the touch.
Drowking lies the meadow-sweet
Flopping down beneath one's feet;
While to all the flow'rs that blow,

If in open air they grow,
Th'injurious deed alike is done
By the hot relentless sun.   50
E'en the dew is parched up
From the teazle's jointed cup. –
O poor birds where must ye fly,
Now your water-pots are dry?
If ye stay upon the heath
Ye'll be chok'd and clamm'd to death,
Therefore leave the shadeless goss,
Seek the spring-head lin'd with moss

There your little feet may stand,
Safely printing on the sand;   60
While in full possession, where
Purling eddies ripple clear,
You with ease and plenty blest,
Sip the coolest and the best;
Then away and wet your throats,
Cheer me with your warbling notes;
'Twill hot Noon the more revive:
While I wander to contrive
For myself a place as good,
In the middle of a wood;   70
There, aside some mossy bank,
Where the grass in bunches rank
Lift it's down on spindles high
Shall be where I'll choose to lie;
Fearless of the things that creep,
There I'll think and there I'll sleep;
Caring not to stir at all,
Till the dew begins to fall.

Composed 1809   First published 1820

THE HARVEST MORNING

Cocks wake the early morn wi' many a Crow
Loud ticking village clock has counted four
The labouring rustic hears his restless foe
And weary bones and pains complaining sore
Hobbles to fetch his horses from the moor
Some busy 'gin to team the loaded corn
Which night throng'd round the barns becrouded door
Such plentious scenes the farmers yards adorn
Such busy bustling toils now mark the harvest morn

The birdboy's pealing horn is loudly blow'd   10
The waggons jostle on wi' rattling sound
And hogs and geese now throng the dusty road
Grunting and gabbling in contension round
The barley ears that litter on the ground –
What printing traces mark the waggons way
What busy bustling wakens echo round
How drives the suns warm beams the mist away
How labour sweats and toils and dreads the sultry day

His scythe the mower oer his shoulder leans
And wetting jars wi' sharp and tinkling sound   20
Then sweeps again 'mong corn and crackling beans
And swath by swath flops lengthening oer the ground
While 'neath some friendly heap snug shelterd round
From spoiling sun lies hid their hearts delight
And hearty soaks oft hand the bottle round
Their toils pursuing with redoubl'd might
Refreshments cordial hail –
Great praise to him be due that brought thy birth to light

Upon the waggon now with eager bound
The lusty picker wirls the rustling sheaves   30
Or ponderous resting creaking fork aground
Boastful at once whole shocks o' barley heaves
The loading boy revengefull inly greaves

To find his unmatch'd strength and power decay
Tormenting <u>horns</u> his garments inter weaves   *bits of barley*
Smarting and sweating 'neath the sultry day
Wi' muttering curses stung he mauls the heaps away

A Motley group the Clearing field surounds
Sons of Humanity O neer deny
The humble gleaner entrance in your grounds   40
Winters sad cold and poverty is nigh
O grudge not providence her scant suply
You'll never miss it from your ample store –
Who gives denial harden'd hungry hound
May never blessings crow'd his hated door
But he shall never lack that giveth to the poor

Ah lovley Ema mingling wi' the rest
Thy beauties blooming in low life unseen
Thy rosey cheeks thy sweetly swelling breast
But ill it suits thee in the stubs to glean   50
O poverty! how basely you demean
The imprison'd worth your rigid fates confine
Not fancied charms of an arcadian queen
So sweet as Emas real beauties shine
Had fortune blest sweet girl this lot had neer been thine

The suns increasing heat now mounted high
Refreshment must recruit exausted power
The waggon stops the busy tools thrown bye
And 'neath a shock's enjoy'd the <u>beavering hour</u>   *meal break*
The bashful maid – sweet healths engaging flower   60
Lingering behind – oer rake still blushing bends
And when to take the horn fond swains implore
With feign'd excuses its dislike pretends
So pass the beavering hours – So harvest morning ends

O rural life what charms thy meaness hide
What sweet descriptions bards disdain to sing

What Loves what Graces on thy plains abide
O could I soar me on the muses wing
What riffel'd charms should my researches bring
Pleas'd would I wander where these charms reside   70
Of rural sports and beauties would I sing
Those beauties wealth which you but vain deride
Beauties of richest bloom superior to your pride

Composed 1818   First published 1820

THE LAMENTATIONS OF
ROUND-OAK WATERS

Oppress'd wi' grief a double share
   Where Round oak waters flow
I one day took a sitting there
   Recounting many a woe
My naked seat without a shade
   Did cold and blealy shine
Which fate was more agreable made
   As sympathising mine

The wind between the north and East
   Blow'd very chill and cold   10
Or coldly blow'd to me at least
   My cloa'hs were thin and old
The grass all dropping wet wi dew
   Low bent their tiney spears
The lowly daise' bended too
   More lowly wi my tears

(For when my wretched state appears
   Hurt friendless poor and starv'd
I never can withold my tears
   To think how I am sarv'd   20
To think how money'd men delight
   More cutting then the storm

To make a sport and prove their might
   O' me a fellow worm)

With arms reclin'd upon my knee
   In mellancholly form
I bow'd my head to misery
   And yielded to the storm
And there I fancied uncontrould
   My sorrows as they flew   30
Unnotic'd as the waters rowl'd
   Where all unnoticed too

But soon I found I was deciev'd
   For waken'd by my Woes
The naked stream of shade bereav'd
   In grievous murmurs rose

'Ah luckless youth to sorrow born
   Shun'd Son of Poverty
The worlds made gamely sport and scorn
   And grinning infamy   40
Unequall'd tho thy sorrows seem
   And great indeed they are
O hear my sorrows for my stream
   You'll find an equal there

'I am the genius of the brook
   And like to thee I moan
By Naiads and by all forsook
   Unheeded and alone
Distress and sorrow quickly proves
   The friend sincere and true   50
Soon as our happines removes
   Pretenders bids adieu

'Here I have been for many a year
   And how My brook has been

How pleasures lately flourish'd here
    Thy self has often seen
The willows waving wi' the wind
    And here and there a thorn
Did please thy Mellancholly mind
    And did My banks adorn   60

'And here the shepherd with his sheep
    And with his lovley maid
Together where these waters creep
    In loitering dalliance play'd
And here the Cowboy lov'd to sit   *cowherd*
    And plate his rushy thongs
And dabble in the fancied pit
    And chase the Minnow throngs

'And when thou didst thy horses tend
    Or drive the ploughmans team   70
Thy mind did natturally bend
    Towards my pleasing stream
And different pleasures fill'd thy breast
    And different thy employ
And different feelings thou possest
    From any other Boy

'The sports which they so dearley lov'd
    Thou could's't not bear to see
And joys which they as joys approv'd
    Ne'er seem'd as joys to thee   80
The joy was thine couldst thou but steal
    From all their Gambols rude
In some lone thicket to consceal
    Thyself in Sollitude

'There didst thou joy and love to sit
    The briars and brakes among
To exercise thy infant wit

40

In fancied tale or song
And there the inscect and the flower
   Would Court thy curious eye   90
To muse in wonder on that power
   Which dwells above the sky

'But now alas my charms are done
   For shepherds and for thee
The Cowboy with his Green is gone
   And every Bush and tree
Dire nakedness oer all prevails
   Yon fallows bare and brown
Is all beset wi' post and rails
   And turned upside down   100

'The gentley curving darksom <u>bawks</u>   *grassy strips separating plowed Fields.*
   That stript the Cornfields o'er
And prov'd the Shepherds daily walks
   Now prove his walks no more
The plough has had them under hand
   And over turnd 'em all
And now along the elting Land
   Poor swains are forc'd to maul

'And where yon furlong meets the lawn
   To Ploughmen Oh! how sweet   110
When they had their long furrow drawn
   Its <u>Eddings</u> to their feet   *grassy strips at ends of plowed fields*
To rest 'em while they clan'd their plough
   And light their Loaded Shoe
But ah – there's ne'er an Edding now
   For neither them nor you

'The bawks and Eddings are no more
   The pastures too are gone
The greens the Meadows and the moors
   Are all cut up and done   120

41

There's scarce a greensward spot remains
   And scarce a single tree
All naked are thy native plains
   And yet they're dear to thee

'But O! my brook my injur'd brook
   'T'is that I most deplore
To think how once it us'd to look
   How it must look no more
And hap'ly fate thy wanderings bent
   To sorrow here wi' me   130
For to none else could I lament
   And mourn to none but thee

'Thou art the whole of musing swains
   That's now resideing here
Tho one ere while did grace my plains
   And he to thee was dear
Ah – dear he was – for now I see
   His Name grieves thee at heart
Thy silence speaks that Misery
   Which Language cant impart   140

'O T—l T—l dear should thou   *Turnhill, the name of a friend*
   To this fond Mourner be
By being so much troubl'd now
   From just a Nameing thee
Nay I as well as he am griev'd
   For oh I hop'd of thee
That hadst thou stay'd as I believd
   Thou wouldst have griev'd for me

'But ah he's gone the first o' swains
   And left us both to moan   150
And thou art all that now remains
   With feelings like his own
So while the thoughtless passes by

Of sence and feelings void
Thine be the Fancy painting Eye
  On by'gone scenes employ'd

'Look backward on the days of yore
  Upon my injur'd brook
In fancy con its Beauties o'er
  How it had us'd to look   160
O then what trees my banks did crown
  What Willows flourished here
Hard as the ax that Cut them down
  The senceless wretches were

'But sweating slaves I do not blame
  Those slaves by wealth decreed
No I should hurt their harmless name
  To brand 'em wi' the deed
Altho their aching hands did wield
  The axe that gave the blow   170
Yet 't'was not them that own'd the field
  Nor plan'd its overthrow

'No no the foes that hurt my field
  Hurts these poor moilers too
And thy own bosom knows and feels
  Enough to prove it true
And o poor souls they may complain
  But their complainings all
The injur'd worms that turn again
  But turn again to fall   180

'Their foes and mine are lawless foes
  And L—ws thems—s they hold
Which clipt-wing'd Justice cant oppose
  But forced [and] yields to G—d
These are the f—s of mine and me
  These all our Ru—n plan'd

Alltho they never felld a tree
  Or took a tool in hand

'Ah cruel foes with plenty blest
  So ankering after more   190
To lay the greens and pastures waste
  Which proffited before
Poor greedy souls – what would they have
  Beyond their plenty given?
Will riches keep 'em from the grave?
  Or buy them rest in heaven?'

Composed 1818   First published 1935

from SUMMER EVENING

The sinken sun is takin leave
And sweetly gilds the edge of eve
While purple [clouds] of deepening dye
Huddling hang the western skye
Crows crowd quaking over head
Hastening to the woods to bed
Cooing sits the lonly dove
Calling home her abscent love
Kirchip Kirchip mong the wheat
Partridge distant partridge greet   10
Beckening call to those that roam
Guiding the squandering covey home
Swallows check their rambling flight
And twittering on the chimney light
Round the pond the martins flirt
Their snowy breasts bedawbd in dirt
While the mason neath the slates
Each morter bearing bird awaits
Untaught by art each labouring spouse
Curious daubs his hanging house   20
Bats flit by in hood and cowl
Thro the barn hole pops the owl

From the hedge the beetles boom
Heedless buz and drousy hum
Haunting every bushy place
Flopping in the labourers face
Now the snail has made his ring
And the moth with snowy wing
Fluttering plays from bent [to bent]
Bending down with dews besprent   30
Then on resting branches hing
Strength to ferry oer the spring
From the haycocks moistend heaps
Frogs now take their Vaunting leaps
And along the shaven mead
Quickly travelling they proceed
[Flying] from their speckled sides
Dewdrops bounce as grass divides
[Now the blue fog creeps along,
And the bird's forgot his song:]   40
Flowrets sleeps within their hoods
Daisys button into buds
From soiling dew the butter cup
Shuts his golden jewels up
And the Rose and woodbine they
Wait again the smiles of day
Neath the willows wavy boughs
Nelly singing milks her cows
While the streamlet bubling bye
Joins in murmuring melody   50
Now the hedger hides his bill
And with his faggot climbs the hill
Driver Giles wi rumbling joll
And blind <u>ball</u> jostles home the roll   οX
Whilom Ralph for doll to wait
Lolls him oer the pasture gate
Swains to fold their sheep begin
Dogs bark loud to drive em in
Ploughmen from their furrowy seams

45

Loose the weary fainting teams   60
Ball wi cirging lashes weald
Still so slow to drive afield
Eager blundering from the plough
Wants no wip to drive him now
At the stable door he stands
Looking round for friendly hands
To loose the door its fastening pin
Ungear him now and let him in
Round the Yard a thousand ways
The beest in expectation gaze   70
Tugging at the loads of hay
As passing fotherers hugs away
And hogs wi grumbling deafening noise
Bother round the server boys
And all around a motly troop
Anxious claim their suppering up
From the rest a blest release
Gabbling goes the fighting geese
Waddling homward to their bed
In their warm straw litterd shed   80
Nighted by unseen delay
Poking hens that loose their way
Crafty cats now sit to watch
Sparrows fighting on the thatch
Dogs lick their lips and wag their tails
When doll brings in the milking pails
With stroaks and pats their welcomd in
And they with looking thanks begin
She dips the milk pail brimming oer
And hides the dish behind the door   90
Prone to mischief boys are met
Gen the heaves the ladders set
Sly they climb and softly tread
To catch the sparrow on his bed
And kill em O in cruel pride
Knocking gen the ladderside

Cursd barbarions pass me by
Come not turks my cottage nigh
Sure my sparrows are my own
Let ye then my birds alone   100
Sparrows come from foes severe
Fearless come yere welcome here
My heart yearns for fates like thine
A sparrows lifes as sweet as mine
To my cottage then resort
Much I love your chirping note
Wi my own hands to form a nest
Ill gi ye shelter peace and rest
Trifling are the deeds ye do
Grait the pains ye undergo   110
Cruel man woud Justice serve
Their crueltys as they deserve
And justest punishment pursue
And do as they to others do
Ye mourning chirpers fluttering here
They woud no doubt be less severe
Foolhardy clown neer grudge the wheat
Which hunger forces them to eat
Your blinded eyes worst foes to you
Neer see the good which sparrows do   120
Did not the sparrows watching round
Pick up the inscet from your grounds
Did not they tend your rising grain
You then might sow – to reap in vain
Thus providence when understood
Her end and aim is doing good
Sends nothing here without its use
Which Ign'rance loads with its abuse
Thus fools despise the blessing sent
And mocks the givers good intent   130
                    [. . .]

Composed 1809–19   First published 1820

MY MARY

Who lives where Beggars rarley speed?
And leads a humdrum life indeed
As none beside herself would lead
     My Mary

Who lives where noises never cease?
And what wi' hogs and ducks and geese
Can never have a minutes peace
     My Mary

Who nearly battl'd to her chin
Bangs down the yard thro thick and thin?   10
Nor picks a road nor cares a pin
     My Mary

Who (save in sunday bib and tuck)
Goes daily (waddling like a duck)
Oer head and ears in grease and muck
     My Mary

Unus'd to pattins or to clogs
Who takes the swill to serve the hogs?
And steals the milk for cats and dogs
     My Mary   20

Who frost and Snow as hard as nails
Stands out o' doors and never fails
To wash up things and scour the pails
     My Mary

Who bussles night and day in short
At all catch jobs of every sort
And gains her mistress' favor for't
     My Mary

48

And who is oft repaid wi praise?
In doing what her mistress says   30
And yielding to her wimmy ways
          My Mary

For theres none apter I believe
At 'creeping up a Mistress' sleve'
Then this low kindred stump of Eve
          My Mary

Who when the baby's all besh—t
To please its mamma kisses it?
And vows no Rose on earths so sweet
          My Mary   40

But when her Mistress is'n't nigh
Who swears and wishes it would die
And pinches it to make it cry
          My Mary

Oh rank deceit! what soul could think –
But gently there revealing ink
– At faults of thine this friend must wink
          My Mary

Who (not without a 'spark o' pride'
Tho strong as Grunters bristly hide)   50
Does keep her hair in papers ty'd?
          My Mary

And mimicking the Gentry's way
Who strives to speak as fine as they?
And minds but every word they say
          My Mary

And who (tho's well bid blind to see
As her to tell ye A from B)

Thinks herself none o' low degree?
　　　My Mary　　　　　　　　　　　　　　　60

Who prates and runs oer silly stuff?
And 'mong the boys makes sport enough
– So ugly, silly droll and ruff
　　　My Mary

Ugly! Muse fo' shame o' thee
What faults art thou a going to see?
In one thats lotted out to be
　　　My Mary

But heedless sayings meaneth nought
Done Innoscent without a thought　　　　　70
We humbly ask thy pardon for't
　　　My Mary

Who low in Stature thick and fat
Turns brown from going without a hat?
Tho not a pin the worse for that
　　　My Mary

Who's laugh'd at too by every whelp
For failings which they cannot help?
But silly fools will laugh and chelp
　　　My Mary　　　　　　　　　　　　　　80

For tho in stature mighty small
And near as thick as thou art tall
That hand made thee that made us all
　　　My Mary

And tho thy nose hooks down too much
And prophecies thy chin to touch
I'm not so nice to look at such
　　　My Mary

No no about thy nose and chin
Its hooking out or bending in   90
I never heed nor care a pin
      My Mary

And tho thy skin is brown and ruff
And form'd by nature hard and tuff
All suiteth me! so thats enough
      My Mary

Composed 1809–19   First published 1820

'GRAMMAR'

[. . .] I thought sometimes that I surely had a taste peculiarly by myself and that nobody else thought or saw things as I did. Still, as my highest ambition at that time was nothing else but the trifle of pleasing one's self, these fancies could dishearten me very little while that gratification was always at hand. But a circumstance occurred which nearly stopped me from writing even for my own amusement. Borrowing a school book of a companion having some entertaining things in it both in prose and verse, with an introduction by the compiler, who doubtless like myself knew little about either (for such like affect to   10
give advice to others while they want it themselves), in this introduction was rules both for writing as well as reading Compositions in prose and verse; where stumbling on a remark that a person who knew nothing of grammar was not capable of writing a letter nor even a bill of parcels, I was quite in the suds, seeing that I had gone on thus far without learning the first rudiments of doing it properly. For I had hardly said the name of grammar while at school.

But as I had an itch for trying at everything I got hold of, I determined to try grammar, and for that purpose, by the   20
advice of a friend, bought the 'Spelling Book' as the most easy assistant for my starting out. But finding a jumble of words classed under this name, and that name and this such-a-figure

51

of speech and that another-hard-worded-figure, I turned from
further notice of it in instant disgust. For, as I knew I coud talk
to be understood, I thought by the same method my writing
might be made out as easy and as proper. So in the teeth of
grammar I pursued my literary journey as warm as usual,
working hard all day and scribbling at night, or any leisure
hour, in any convenient hole or corner I could shove in unseen;   30
for I always carried a pencil in my pocket, having once bought
at Stamford Fair a dozen of a Jew for a shilling, which lasted
me for years.

Till necessity, as I got up towards manhood, urged me to
look for something more than pleasing one's self, my poems
had been kept with the greatest industry under wish'd
concealment, having no choice to gratify by their disclosure,
but on the contrary, chilling damp with fear, whenever I
thought of it. The laughs and jeers of those around me, when
they found out I was a poet, was present death to my ambitious   40
apprehensions; for in our unlettered villages, the best of the
inhabitants have little more knowledge in reading than what
can be gleaned from a weekly Newspaper, Old Moore's
Almanack, and a Prayer Book on Sundays at Church, while the
labouring classes remain as blind in such matters as the Slaves in
Africa. [. . .]

Composed 1821   First published 1931

SUMMER

How sweet when weary dropping on a bank
Turning a look around on things that be
Een feather headed grasses spindling rank
A trembling to the breeze one loves to see
And yellow buttercups where many a bee
Comes buzzing to its head and bows it down
And the great dragon flye wi gauzy wings
In gilded coat of purple green or brown
That on broad leaves of hazel basking clings

Fond of the sunny day – and other things   10
Past counting pleases one while thus I lye
But still reflective pains are not forgot
Summer somtime shall bless this spot when I
Hapt in the cold dark grave can heed it not

Composed 1819–21   First published 1821

PROPOSALS FOR
BUILDING A COTTAGE

Beside a runnel build my shed
Wi' stubbles coverd oer
Let broad oaks oer its chimley spread
And grass plats grace the door

The door may open wi a string
So that it closes tight
And locks too woud be wanted things
To keep out thieves at night

A little garden not too fine
Inclosed wi painted pails   10
And wood bines round the cot to twine
Pind to the wall wi nails

Let hazels grow and spindling sedge
Bent bowering over head
Dig old mans beard from woodland hedge
To twine a summer shade

Beside the threshold sods provide
And build a summer seat
Plant sweet briar bushes by its side
And flowers that smelleth sweet   20

I love the sparrows ways to watch
Upon the cotters sheds
So here and there pull out the thatch
As they may hide their heads

And as the sweeping swallows stop
Their flights along the green
Leave holes within the chimney top
To paste their nest between

Stick shelves and cupboards round the hut
In all the holes and nooks   30
Nor in the corner fail to put
A cubboard for the books

Along the floor some sand Ill sift
To make it fit to live in
And then Ill thank ye for the gift
As somthing worth the giving

Composed 1819–21   First published 1821

LANGLEY BUSH

O Langley bush the shepherds sacred shade
Thy hollow trunk oft gaind a look from me
Full many a journey oer the heath ive made
For such like curious things I love to see
What truth the story of the swain alows
That tells of honours which thy young days knew
Of 'langley court' being kept beneath thy boughs
I cannot tell – thus much I know is true
That thou art reverencd even the rude clan
Of lawless gipseys drove from stage to stage   10
Pilfering the hedges of the husband man
Leave thee as sacred in thy withering age
Both swains and gipseys seem to love thy name

54

Thy spots a favourite wi the smutty crew
And soon thou must depend on gipsey fame
Thy mulldering trunk is nearly rotten thro
My last doubts murmuring on the zephers swell
My last looks linger on thy boughs wi pain
To thy declining age I bid farwell
Like old companions neer to meet again   20

Composed 1819—21   First published 1821

THE WOODMAN

The beating snow clad bell wi sounding dead
Hath clanked four – the woodmans wakd agen
And as he leaves his comfortable bed
Dithers to view the ryhmey featherd pane
And shrugs and wishes – but its all in vain
The beds warm comforts he must now forgo
His family that oft till eight hath lain
Wi out his labours wage coud not do so
And glad to make them blest he shoffles thro the snow

The early winters morns as dark as pitch   10
The warey wife keeps tinder every night
Wi flint and steal and many a sturdy twitch
Sits up in bed to strike her man a light
And as the candle shows the rapturous sight
Aside his wife his rosey sleeping boy
He smacks his lips wi exquisite delight
Wi all a fathers feelings fathers joy
Then bids his wife good bye and hies to his employ

His breakfast water porridge humble food
A barley crust he in his wallet flings   20
Wi this he toils and labours i' the wood
And chops his faggot twists his band and sings
As happily as princes and as kings

55

Wi all their luxury – and blest is he
Can but the little which his labour brings
Make both ends meet and from long debts keep free
And keep as neat and clean his creasing family

Far oer the dreary fields the woodland lies
Rough is the journey which he daily goes
The wooley clouds that hang the frowning skies   30
Keep winnowing down their drifting sleet and snows
And thro his doublet keen the north wind blows
While hard as iron the cemented ground
As smooth as glass the glibbed pool is froze
His nailed boots wi clenching tread rebound
And dithering echo starts and mocks the clamping sound

The woods how gloomy in a winters morn
The crows and ravens even cease to croak
The little birds sit chittering on the thorn
The pies scarce chatter when they leave the oak   40
Startld from slumber by the woodmans stroke
The milk maids songs is drownd in gloomy care
And while the village chimleys curl their smoke
She milks and blows and hastens to be there
And nature all seems sad and dying in despair

The squirking rabbit scarcly leaves her hole
But rolls in torpid slumbers all the day
The fox is loath to gin a long patrole
And scouts the woods content wi meaner prey
The hare so frisking timid once and gay   50
Hind the dead thistle hurkles from the view
Nor scarcely scard tho in the travellers way
Tho waffling curs and shepherd dogs pursue
So winters riggid power affects all nature through

What different changes winters frowns supplies
The clown no more a loitering hour beguiles

56

Nor gauping tracks the clouds along the skyes
As when buds blossom and the warm sun smiles
When lawrence wages bids on hills and stiles
Banks stiles and flowers and skyes no longer charm   60
Deep snow and ice each summer seat defiles
Wi hasty blundering step and folded arm
He glad the stable seeks his frost nipt nose to warm

The shepherd seeks no more his spreading oak
Nor on the sloping pond head lyes at lare
The arbour he once wattld up is broke
And left unworthy of his future care
The ragged plundering stickers have bin there
And bottld it away – he passes bye
His summer dwelling desolate and bare   70
And neer so much as turns a 'serning eye   *discerning*
But gladly seeks his fire and leaves the 'clement skye   *inclement*

The scenes all clothd in snow from morn till night
The woodmans loath his chilly tools to sieze
The crows unroosting as he comes in sight
Shake down the feathery burthen from the trees
To look at things around hes fit to freeze
Scard from her pearch the fluttering pheasant flies
His coat and hat wi ryhme is turned white
He quakes looks round and pats his hands and sighs   80
And wishes to him self that the warm sun woud rise

And be the winter cutting as it will
Let north winds winnow fit to nip one through
In the deep woods hard fate demands him still
To stand the bitterest blasts that ever blew
Where trees instead of leaves and pearly dew
In ryhme and snow and Iscicles abound
The proverb 'use is second natures' true
It must be so or how coud he be found
To weather out the blast and daily stand his ground   90

And yet tho fortune frowns upon the poor
And dooms their life to slavish hard employ
Tho wealth forever gainst em shuts her door
And strives their fainting wishes to destroy
Yet still poor souls they have a glimpse of joy
A sugard charm still sweets the sours of fate
His sparing bliss when met does never cloy
While over much does paul the idly great
As rich and sumptious foods does surfeitings create

Good luck it is his providential wealth   100
That hardy labour and the freshning air
Shoud 'crease his strength and keep entire his health
And neer let illness on his soul despair
Wi wife and childern pending on his care
What woud he do a livlihood to gain
The parish moneys but a pining fare
Such scant benevolence he does disdain
Who grudges what they give and mocks the poor mans pain

But if unwell from toil hes forcd to stop
He quickly then repairs to medcines aid   110
Tho not to nauciates of the druggists shop
Or cant advice of docters mystic trade
But to such drugs as daily are displayd
Een round his walks and cottage door profuse
'Self heal' and 'agrimony' which has made   *wild flowers*
Full many an huswife wonderous cures produce
These he in summer seeks and hurds up for his use

The robin tamest of the featherd race
Soon as he hears the woodmans sounding chops
Wi ruddy bosom and a simple face   120
Around his old companions feet he hops
And there for hours in pleasd attention stops
The woodmans heart is tender and humane
And at his meals he many a crumble drops

Thanks to thy generous feelings gentle swain
And what thy pity gives shall not be gave in vain

The woodman pleased views the closing day
To see the sun drop down behind the wood
Sinking in clouds deep blue or misty grey
Round as a football and as red as blood   130
The pleasing prospect does his heart much good
Tho tis not his such beautys to admire
He hastes to fill his bags wi billet wood
Well pleasd from the chill prospect to retire
To seek his corner chair and warm snug cottage fire

And soon the dusky even hovers round
And the white frost gins crizzle pond and brook
The little family are squinting round
And from the door dart many a wistful look
The suppers ready stewing on the hook   140
And every foot that clampers down the street
Is for the coming fathers step mistook
And joyd are they when he their eyes does meet
Bent neath his load snow clad as whites a sheet

I think I see him seated in his chair
Taking the bellows up the fire to blow
I think I hear him joke and chatter there
Telling his childern news they wish to know
Wi leather leggings on that stopt the snow
His broad brimd hat uncoothly shapen round   150
Nor woud he Ill be bound woud it were so
Gi two pence for the chance did it abound
At that same hour to be the king of england crownd

Soons suppers down the thrifty wife seeks out
Her little jobs of family conserns
Chiding her children rabbling about
Says theyll 'stroy more then what their father earns

And their torn clohs she bodges up and darns
For desent women cannot bear the sight
Of dirty houses and of ragged bairns   160
Tis their employment and their chief delight
To keep their cots and childern neat and tight

The woodman smokes the brats in mirth and glee
And artless prattle evens hours beguile
While <u>love's last pledge</u> runs scrambling up his knee   *youngest child*
The nightly comfort from his weary toil
His chuff cheeks dimpling in a fondling smile
He claims his kiss and says his scraps of prayer
Begging his daddys pretty song the while
Playing wis jacket buttons and his hair   170
And thus in wed locks joys the labourer drowns his care

Nor can one miss the bliss from labour freed
Which poor men meeteth on a Sunday morn
Fixt in a chair some godly book to read
Or wandering round to view the crops and corn
In best cloaths fitted out and beard new shorn
Dropping adown in some warm shelterd dell
Wi six days labour weak and weary worn
Listning around each distant chiming bell
That on the softening air melodiously doth swell   180

His pipe pufft out he edges in his chair
And stirs the embers up his hands to warm
And with his singing book he does repair
To humming oer an anthem hymn or psalm
Nor does he think a ballad any harm
But often carrols oer his cottage hearth
'Bold robin hood' the 'Shipwreck' or the 'storm'
O where we find this social joy and mirth
There we may truly say a heaven exists on earth

60

The clock when eight warns all for bed prepare   190
The children still an extra minute crave
And sawn and stammer longer oer their prayers
And they such tempting fond excuses have
The 'dulging father oft the boon has gave
And sung again the younkers to delight
While every hard earnd farden glad to save
The carfull wife puts out the candle light
And oer the fire the song and tale makes sweet the winters
   night

And as most lab'rers knowingly pretend
By certain signs to judge the weather right   200
As oft from 'noahs ark' great floods desend
And 'burred moons' fortell great storms at night   *ring around the*
In such like things the wood man took delight   *moon*
And ere he went to bed woud always ken
Wether the sky was gloomd or stars shone bright
Then went to comforts arms till morn and then
As cheery as the sunrise beams resumd his toils agen

And ere he slept he always breathd a prayer
'I thank thee lord what thou to day didst give
Sufficient strength to toil I bless thy care   210
And thank thee still for what I may recieve
And o almighty god while I still live
My eyes if opend on the last days sun
Prepare thou me this wicked world to leave
And fit my passage ere my race is run
Tis all I beg o lord thy heavenly will be done'

Holland to thee this humble ballads sent
Thee who for poor mans well fare oft hath prayd
Whose tongue did neer belye its good intent
Preacher as well in practice as in trade   220
Alas too often moneys business made

Holland: name of a friend, a Congretational minister

61

O may the wretch thats still on darkness living
The bibles comforts hear by thee displayd
And many a woodmans family forgiven
Have cause for blessing thee that led their way for heaven

Composed 1819–21   First published 1821

CHILDISH RECOLLECTIONS   *p, 229*

Each scene of youth to mes a pleasing toy
Which memory like a lover doats upon
And mixt wi them I am again a boy
And tears and sighs regret the things thats gone

Ah wi enthusiast excesses wild
The scenes of childhood meet my moistning eye
And wi the very weakness of a child
I feel the raptures of delights gone bye

And if Im childish wi such trifling things
If littleness it shows and vain and weak   10
When such-like foolishness in memory springs
Vain as it is I cannot help but speak

And still I fancy as around I stroll
Each boyish scene to mark the sport and game
Theres others living wi a self-like soul
That thinks and loves such trifles just the same

An old familiar spot I witness here
Wi young companions were we oft have met   *where*
Tho since we playd tis bleachd wi many a year
The sports as warmly thrills my bosom yet   20

                         where
Here winds the dyke were oft we jumpt across
Tis just as if it were but yesternight

There hangs the gate we call'd our wooden horse
Were we in swee-swaw ridings took delight

See-saw

And every thing shines round me just as then
Mole hills and trees and bushes speckling wild
That freshens all those pastimes up agen
O grievous day that changd me from a child

To seek the play thing and the pleasing toy
The painted pootey shell and summer flowers
How blest was I when I was here a boy
What joys were mine in these delightfull hours

snail 30

On this same bank I bound my poseys up
And culld the sweetest blossoms one by one
The cowslips still entices me to stoop
But all the feelings they inspird are gone

Tho in the midst of each endeard delight
Where still the cowslaps to the breezes bow
Tho all my childish scenes are in my sight
Sad manhood marks me an intruder now

40

Here runs the brook which I have damd and stopt
Wi choaking sods and water weeds and stones
And watchd wi joy till bursting off it plopt
In rushing gushes of wild murmering groans

Here stands the tree wi clasping ivy bound
Which oft I've clumb to see the chaps at plough
And checkerd fields for many a furlong round
Rock'd by the winds upon its topmost bough

Ah on this bank how blest I once have felt
When here I sat and mutterd namless songs
And wi the shepherd boy and netterd knelt
Upon yon rush beds plaiting whips and thongs

cowherd 50

Fond memory warms as here with gravel shells
I pil'd my fancied cots and wall'd rings
And scoopt wi wooden knife my little wells
And fill'd em up wi water from the springs

cottages

Ah memory sighs now hope my heart beguiles
To build as yet snug cots to cheer despair
While fate at distance mocks wi grining smiles
And calls my structures castles in the air

60

Now een the thistles quaking in the wind
The very rushes nodding o'er the green
Hold each expressive language to my mind
That like old mayteys tell of what has been

*companions
(mates)*

O 'sweet of sweets' from infancy that flow
When can we witness bliss so sweet as then
Might I but have my choice of joy below
I'd only ask to be a boy agen

Life owns no joy so pleasant as the past
That banish'd pleasure rapt in memory's womb
It leaves a flavour sweet to every taste
Like the sweet substance of the honey comb

70

Composed 1819–21   First published 1821

WRITTEN IN NOVEMBER

Autumn I love thy latter end to view
In cold november's day so bleak and bare
When like life's dwindld thread worn nearly thro
Wi lingering pottering pace and head bleachd bare
Thou like an old man bids the world adieu
I love thee well and often when a child
Have roamd the bare brown heath a flower to find
And in the moss-clad vale and wood bank wild

Have cropt the little bell flowers paley blue
That trembling peept the sheltering bush behind   10
When winnowing north winds cold and <u>blealy</u> blew   *bleakly*
How have I joyd wi <u>dithering</u> hands to find   *shivering*
Each fading flower and still how sweet the blast
Woud bleak november's hour Restore the joy that's past

Composed 1819–21   First published 1821

THE GIPSEYS CAMP   *p. 229*

How oft on Sundays when Id time to tramp
My rambles led me to a gipseys' camp
Where the real effegies of midnight hags
Wi tawney smoaked flesh and tatterd rags
Uncooth brimd hat and weather-beaten cloak
'Neath the wild shelter of a <u>notty</u> oak   *knotty*
Along the greensward uniformly pricks
Her pliant bending hazels arching sticks
While round-topt bush or briar-entangld hedge
Where'neath broad flag leaves spring or ramping sedge   10
Keep off the bothering bustle of the wind
And give the best retreat they hope to find
How oft Ive bent me oer their fire and smoak
To hear their gibberish tale so quaintly spoke
While the old sybil forcd her boding <u>clack</u>
Twin imps the mean while bawling at her back
Oft on my hand her magic coins bin struck
And hoping chink she talkd of <u>morts</u> of luck   *lots*
And still as boyish hopes did erst agree
Mingld wi fears to drop the fortunes fee   20
I never faild to gain the honours sought
And Lord and Squire was purchasd wi a groat
But as mans unbelieving taste came round
She furious stampt her shooless foot aground
Wipd by her sut-black hair wi clenching fist
       soot

65

While thro her yellow teeth the spittle hist
Swearing by all her lucky powers of fate
That like as foot boys on her actions wait
That fortunes scale shoud to my sorrow turn
And I one day the rash neglect shoud mourn   30
That good to bad shoud change and I shoud be
Lost to this world and all eternity
That poor as Job I shoud remain unblest
Alas for fourpence how my dye is cast
Of neer a <u>hurded</u> <u>farding</u> be possest   *hoarded farthing*
And when alls done be shovd to hell at last

Composed 1819–21   First published 1821

'MY FIRST ATTEMPTS AT POETRY'

I NOW followd gardening for a while in the Farmers' Gardens
about the village & workd in the fields when I had no other
employment to go to. Poetry was a troublesomely pleasant
companion annoying & cheering me at my toils I coud not stop
my thoughts & often faild to keep them till night so when I
fancyd I had hit upon a good image or natural description I usd
to steal into a corner of the garden & clap it down but the
appearance of my employers often put my fancys to flight &
made me loose the thought & the music together for I always
felt anxiety to control my scribbling & woud as leave have   10
confessd to be a robber as a ryhmer when I workd in the fields I
had more oppertunitys to set down my thoughts & for that
reason I liked to work in the fields & bye & bye forsook
gardening altogether till I resumd it at Casterton I usd to drop
down behind a hedge bush or dyke & write down my things
upon the crown of my hat & when I was more in a <u>kip</u> for   *mood*
thinking than usual I usd to stop later at night to make up my
lost time in the day thus I went on writing my thoughts down
& correcting them at leisure spending my Sundays in the
woods or heaths to be alone for that purpose & I got a bad   20
name among the weekly church goers, forsaking the

churchgoing bell & seeking the religion of the fields tho I did it
for no dislike to church for I felt uncomfortable very often but
my heart burnt over the pleasures of solitude & the restless
revels of ryhme that was eternally sapping my memorys like
the summer sun over the tinkling brook till it one day shoud
leave them dry & unconscious of the thrilling joys busy
anxietys & restlessness which it had created & the praises &
censures which I shall leave behind me I knew nothing of the
poets experience then or I shoud have remaind a labourer & not   30
livd to envy the ignorance of my old companions & fellow
clowns I wish I had not known any other tho I was not known   *laborers*
as a poet my odd habits did not escape notice they fancyd I kept
aloof for some sort of study others believd me crazd & some
put more criminal interpretations to my rambles & said I was
night-walking associating with the gipseys robbing the woods
of the hares & pheasants because I was often in their company
& I must confess I found them far more honest than their
calumniators whom I knew to be of that description Scandel &
Fame are cheaply purchasd in a village the first is a nimble-   40
tongued gossip & the latter a credulous & ready believer who
woud not hesitate but believd anything I had got the fame of
being a good scholar & in fact I had vanity enough to fancy I
was far from a bad one myself while I coud puzzle the village
schoolmaster over my quart (for I had no tongue to brag with
till I was inspired with ale) with solving algebra questions for I
had once struggled hard to get fame in that crabbed wilderness
but my brain was not made for it & it woud not reach it tho it
was a mystery only half unveild to my capacity yet I made
enough of it to astonish their ignorance, for a village   50
schoolmaster is one of the most pretending & most ignorant of
men [. . .]

Composed 1824   First published 1951

from THE VILLAGE MINSTREL

As most of nature's children prove to be,
His little soul was easy made to smart,
His tear was quickly born to sympathy,   210
And soon were rous'd the feelings of his heart
In others' woes and wants to bear a part.
Yon parish-huts, where want is shov'd to die,
He never view'd them but his tear would start;
He pass'd not by the doors without a sigh,
And felt for every woe of workhouse-misery.

O Poverty! thy frowns were early dealt
O'er him who mourn'd thee, not by fancy led
To whine and wail o'er woes he never felt,
Staining his rhymes with tears he never shed,   220
And heaving sighs a mock song only bred:
Alas! he knew too much of every pain
That shower'd full thick on his unshelter'd head;
And as his tears and sighs did erst complain,
His numbers took it up, and wept it o'er again.   *poems*

Full well might he his early days recall,
When he a thresher with his sire has been,
When he a ploughboy in the fields did maul,   *drag along wearily*
And drudg'd with toil through almost every scene;
How pinch'd with winter's frownings he has been;   230
And tell of all that modesty conceals,
Of what his friends and he have felt and seen:
But, useless naming what distress reveals,
As every child of want feels all that Lubin feels.

It might be curious here to hint the lad,
How in his earliest days he did appear;
Mean was the dress in which the boy was clad,
His friends so poor, and clothes excessive dear,
They oft were foil'd to rig him once a year;   *outfit*

And housewife's care in many a patch was seen;   240
Much industry 'gainst want did persevere;
His friends tried all to keep him neat and clean,
Though care has often fail'd, and shatter'd he has been.

Yet oft fair prospects cheer'd his parents' dreams,
Who had on Lubin founded many a joy;
But pinching want soon baffled all their schemes,
And dragg'd him from the school a hopeless boy,
To shrink unheeded under hard employ;
When struggling efforts warm'd him up the while,
To keep the little toil could not destroy;   250
And oft with books spare hours he would beguile,
And blunder oft with joy round Crusoe's lonely isle.

Folks much may wonder how the thing may be,
That Lubin's taste should seek refinèd joys,
And court th'enchanting smiles of poesy;
Bred in a village full of strife and noise,
Old senseless gossips, and blackguarding boys,
Ploughmen and threshers, whose discourses led
To nothing more than labour's rude employs,
'Bout work being slack, and rise and fall of bread,   260
And who were like to die, and who were like to wed:

Housewives discoursing 'bout their hens and cocks,
Spinning long stories, wearing half the day,
Sad deeds bewailing of the prowling fox,
How in the roost the thief had knav'd his way
And made their market-profits all a prey.
And other losses too the dames recite,
Of chick, and duck, and gosling gone astray,
All falling prizes to the <u>swopping kite</u>:   *swooping, bird of prey*
And so the story runs both morning, noon, and night.   270

Nor sabbath-days much better thoughts instil;
The true-going churchman hears the signal ring,

And takes his book his homage to fulfil,
And joins the clerk his amen-task to sing,
And rarely home forgets the text to bring:
But soon as service ends, he 'gins again
'Bout signs in weather, late or forward spring,
Of prospects good or bad in growing grain;
And if the sermon's long he waits the end with pain.

A more uncouthly lout was hardly seen   280
Beneath the shroud of ignorance than he;
The sport of all the village he has been,
Who with his simple looks oft jested free;
And gossips, gabbling o'er their cake and tea,
Time after time did prophecies repeat,
How half a ninny he was like to be,
To go so <u>soodling</u> up and down the street   *dawdling*
And shun the playing boys whene'er they chanc'd to meet.

Nature look'd on him with a 'witching eye,
Her pleasing scenes were his delightful book,   290
Where <u>Were</u> he, while other louts roam'd heedless by,
With wild enthusiasm us'd to look.
The kingcup vale, the gravel-paved brook,
Were paradise with him to muse among;
And haply sheltering in some lonely nook,
He often sat to see it purl along,
And, fir'd with what he saw, humm'd o'er his simple song.

When summer came, how eager has he sped
Where silence reign'd, and the old crownèd tree
Bent with its sheltering ivy o'er his head;   300
And summer-breezes, breathing placidly,
Encroach'd upon the <u>stockdove</u>'s privacy,   *a bird*
Parting the leaves that screen'd her russet breast:
'Peace!' would he whisper, 'dread no thief in me,'
And never rose to rob her careless nest;
Compassion's softness reign'd, and warm'd his gentle breast.

And he would trace the stagnant pond or lake,
Where <u>flags</u> sprang up or water-lilies smil'd,   rushes
And wipe the boughs aside of bush and <u>brake</u>,   bracken
And creep the woods with sweetest scenes beguil'd,   310
Tracking some channel on its journey wild,
Where dripping blue-bells on the bank did weep:
Oh, what a lovely scene to nature's child,
Through roots and o'er dead leaves to see it creep,
Watching on some moss'd stump in contemplation deep.

Composed 1819–21   First published 1821

HELPSTON GREEN

Ye injur'd fields ere while so gay
When natures hand display'd
Long waving rows of Willows gray
And clumps of Hawthorn shade
But now alas your <u>awthorn</u> bowers   hawthorn
All desolate we see
The tyrant's hand their shade devours
And cuts down every tree

Not tree's alone have felt their force
Whole Woods beneath them bow'd   10
They stopt the winding runlets course
And flowrey pastures plough'd
To shrub nor tree throughout thy fields
They no compasion show
The uplifted ax no mercy yields
But strikes a fatal blow

When ere I muse along the plain
And mark where once they grew
Rememberance wakes her busy train
And brings past scenes to view   20
The well known brook the favorite tree

In fancy's eye appear
And next that pleasant green I see
That green for ever dear

O'er its green hill's I've often stray'd
In Childhood's happy hour
Oft sought the nest along the shade
And gather'd many a flower
With fellow play mates often joind
In fresher sports to plan   30
But now encreasing years have coind
This play mate into man

The green's gone too ah lovly scene
No more the king cup gay
Shall shine in yellow oer the green
And add a golden ray
Nor more the herdsman's early call
Shall bring the cows to feed
Nor more the milk maids awkard brawl
Bright echo in the mead   40

Both milkmaids shouts and herdsmans call
Have vanish'd with the green
The king kups yellow shades and all
Shall never more be seen
For all the cropping that does grow
Will so efface the scene
That after times will hardly know
It ever was a green

Farwell delightful spot farwell   Farewell
Since every effort's vain   50
All I can do is still to tell
Of thy delightful plain
But that proves short – increasing years
That did my youth presage

72

When every new year's day appears
Will mellow into age

When age resumes the faultering tongue
Alas there's nought can save
Take one more step then all along
We drop into the grave   60
Reflection pierces deadly keen
While I the morral scan   moral
As are the changes of the green
So is the life of man

Composed 1819–21   First published 1821

NOON

The mid day hour of twelve the clock counts oer
A sultry stillness lulls the air asleep
The very buzz of flye is heard no more
Nor one faint wrinkle oer the waters creep
Like one large sheet of glass the pool does shine
Reflecting in its face the burnt sun beam
The very fish their sturting play decline
Seeking the willow shadows side the stream
And where the awthorn branches oer the pool
The little bird forsaking song and nest   10
Flutters on dripping twigs his limbs to cool
And splashes in the stream his burning breast
O free from thunder for a sudden shower
To cherish nature in this noon day hour

Composed 1819–21   First published 1821

from RURAL EVENING

At even's hour the truce of toil tis sweet
The sons of labour at their ease to meet
On piled bench beside the cottage door
Made up of mud and stones and sodded oer
Where Were rustic taste at leisure trimly weaves
The rose and straggling woodbines to the eaves   100
And on the crouded spot that pails enclose   *fences*
The white and scarlet daisey rears in rows
And trailing peas in bunches training neat
Perfuming even with a luscious sweet
And sun flowers planting for their gilded show
That scale the windows lattice ere they blow
And sweet to 'habitants within the sheds
Peep thro the diamond pane their golden heads
Or black smith's shop were ploughs and harrows lye
Well known to every child that passes bye   110
By shining shares that litter on the floor   *plowshares*
And branded letters burnt upon the door
And hard burnt cinders flung as usless bye
That year by year in some spare corner lye
Were meddling boys their ready weapons meet
To pelt each other up and down the street
Or aught that pleases each mischievous eye
As harmless hogs and bullocks passing bye
Or squatting martins neath the eves at rest   *eaves*
That oft are wakd to mourn a ruind nest   120
And sparrows now that love their nests to leave
In dust to flutter at the cool of eve
For such like scenes the gossip leaves her home
And sons of labour light their pipes and come
To talk of wages wether high or low
And mumbld news that still as secrets go
                    [. . .]

Composed c. 1821   First published 1821

74

'GOING FOR A SOLDIER'

[. . .] WHEN the country was chin-deep in the fears of invasion & every month was filled with the terrors which Bonaparte had spread in other countries a national scheme was set on foot to raise a raw army of volunteers, & to make the matter plausible a letter was circulated said to be written by the prince regent. I forget how many was demanded from our parish but I remember the panic which it created was very great. no great name rises in the world without creating a crowd of little mimics that glitter in borrowed rays & no great lie was ever put into circulation with[out] a herd of little lyes multiply[ing] by instinct as it were & crowding under its wings. the papers that were circulated assured the people of England that the French were on the eve of invading it & that it was deemed nessesary by the regent that an army from 18 to 45 should be raised immediately. this was the great lye & the little lies were soon at its heels, which assured the people of Helpstone that the French had invaded & got to London & some of these little lyes had the impudence to swear that the french had even reached northampton. the people got at their doors in the evening to talk over the rebellion of '45 when the rebels reached Derby & even listened at intervals to fancy they heard the french 'rebels' at Northampton knocking it down with their cannon. I never gave much credit to popular storys of any sort so I felt no concern at these storys though I coud not say much for my valour if the tale had provd true. we had a cross-graind sort of choice left us, which was to be forced to be drawn & go for nothing or take on as volunteers for a bounty of two guineas. I accepted the latter & went with a neighbour's son W. Clarke to Peterbrough to be sworn on & prepard to join the regiment at Oundle. the morning we left home our mothers parted with us as if we were going to Botany Bay & people got at their doors to bid us farewell & greet us with a Job's comfort that they doubted we should see Helpstone no more. I confess I wished myself out of the matter by times. when we got to Oundle, the place of quartering, we were drawn out

10

20 1745

30

'45: Jacobin rebellion of 1745
Botany Bay: in Australia, where convicted
    criminals were transported to.

75

into the fields & a more motley multitude of lawless fellows
was never seen in Oundle before & hardly out of it there were
1300 of us we was drawn up into a line & sorted into companys.
I was one of the shortest & therefore my station is evident I was
in that mixed multitude called the batallion which they
nicknamed 'bum-tools', for what reason I cannot tell the light
company was called 'light-bobs' & the grenadiers 'bacon-
bolters' these were names given to each other who felt as great
an enmity against each other as ever they all felt for the french
[. . .]

Composed 1824   First published 1951

from THE FATE OF GENIUS

'I knew him from a child' the clerk woud say
'And often noticd his dislike to play   40
Oft met him then lone left by woods and streams
Muttering about as people do in dreams
And neath lone bushes dropt about the field
Or peacfull hedges that woud shelter yield
With hand beneath his head in silence bent
Oft saw him sit and wonderd what it meant
Nor did his habits alter with his age
Still woods and fields his leisure did engage
Nor friends nor labour woud his thoughts beguile
Still dumb he seemd in company and toil   50
And if ones questions did his dreams supprise
His unconscern oft pausd in wrong replys
We wonderd many times as well we might
And doubted often if his mind was right
Een childern startld from his oddness ran
And shund his wanderings as 'the crazy man'
Tho harmless as the things he mixd among
His ways was gentle and unknown to wrong
For ive oft markd his pity passing bye
Disturb the spiders web to save the flye   60

76

And saw him give to tyrant boys a fee
To buy the captive sparrows liberty
Each sundays leisure brought the woods their guest
And wildest spot which suited him the best
As bushy greens and valleys left untilld
where Were weedy brooks went crooking as they willd
Were flags and reeds and sedge disorderd grew
These woud his abscence from his home pursue
And as he rambld in each peacful round
Hed fancy friends in every thing he found   70
Muttering to cattle – aye and even flowers
As one in visions claimd his talk for hours
And hed oft wonder were we nought coud see
On blades of grass and leaves upon the tree
And pointed often in a wild supprise
To trifling hues of gadding butterflys
While if another made new marvels known
That seemd to me far wonderous then his own   *than*
Of ghosts hed seen that nightly walks decievd
He heeded not but laughd and disbelievd   80
Nights dismal tongues that hardest hearts affright
And all may hear that travel out at night
Her shadowd howling tenants fierce and grim
Tho trifles struck him – such was nought to him
At length twas known his ways by woods and brooks
Were secret walks for making ryhmes and books
Which strangers bought and with amazment read
And calld him poet when they sought his shed
But men they said like serpents in the grass
That skulk in ways which learning has to pass   90
To slander worth which they woud feign posses
And dissapointment urges to suppress
Snarling at faults too bright for common minds
And hiding beautys wisdom warmly finds
Such marr'd his powers and slanderd in disguise
And tryd to black his merits with their lyes
And tho his friends the cheating fraud descryd

It hurt too earnest to be wipd aside
He dwindld down from too severe a blast
And hopes might wish to live that dyd as fast   100
Still he did live till real life seemd as gone
And his soul lingerd in a shadowd one
And yet he mingld in his favour ways
And bar'd his forhead to the sunny days
Listning the lark on fountains moaning wave
As like a ghost as ever left its grave
And fled the world at last without a sigh
And dyd as gentle as a lamb woud dye
His learned friends said envy's aim was blest
That malice killd him – they might know the best   110
                [. . .]'

Composed c. 1821   First published 1935

A PROPHET IS NOTHING IN HIS OWN COUNTRY

Envy was up at my success with all the lyes it could muster,
some said that I never wrote the poems & that Drury gave me
money to father them with my name, others said that I had
stole them out of books & that Parson this & Squire tother
knew the books from which they were stolen, Pretending
scholars said that I had never been to a grammer school &
therefore it was impossible for me to write anything, our
parson industriously found out the wonderful discovery that I
coud not spell & of course his opinion was busily distributed in
all companies which he visited that I was but a middling   10
promise of success but his opinion got its knuckles rapt & then
he excusd the mistake by saying he did not read poetry &
consequently knew little about it, there he was right.

    the same prophet caught me working a common problem in
geometry with the scale & compasses in which I was very fond
to dabble, & after expressing his supprise at my meddlings in
such matters he said we do these things different at Colledge;
we make a circle without compasses & work a problem

without a scale – the solution of this problem was something
like a round lye – an old Leicestershire farmer & his family in   20
a neighbouring village was uncommonly against me, they
declard it was impossible for me to do anything & disbelievd
everything but that which was against me – thus every kind
loves its own color & on that principal the Indian believes the
devil a white spirit & the europeans a black one – the old man
had a lubberly son whom he fancied to make a learned one by
sending him to school till he was a man & his ten years wisdom
consisted of finding that 2 & 2 makes 4, that a circle was round
& a triangle had 3 corners & that poetry was nothing in com-
parison, the old man believd & thought likewise   30

My acquaintance with books is not so good as late oppertunity might have made it, for I never coud plod through every
book in a regular mecanical way as I met it, I dip into it here &
there & if it does not suit I lay it down & seldom take it up
again, but in the same manner I read Thomson's *Seasons* &
Milton's *Paradise Lost* thro when I was a boy & they are the
only books of poetry that I have regularly read thro [. . .]

Composed 1824   First published 1951

   from WINTER

Nature that pauses nearly dumb
But startles some complaint to make   90
Not like the buried busyed hum
Which banishd summer kept awake –
here Were sheep their bleating wants reveal
And hollow noise of bawling cow
That wait the fodderers' stinted meal
Is all ones walks can listen now

Save when some clown with beatle breaks   *laborer   hammer*
The ponds thick ice for stock to drink
Wild noises round the village wakes

79

From geese that gabble on the brink 100
Who mope and brood about the snows
When frost their plashy sport destroys *splashy*
Till such scant chance relief bestows
To urge afresh their squalling joys

Oft oer one flyes the chirping lark
With ryhme hung round his chilly breast
Complaining of some dog's rude bark
That scard him from his chilly rest
And oft from snowbanks ridgy edge
The hare steps hirpling oer the plain *limping* 110
Till found a bush or bunch of sedge
Then drops its ears and squats again

And feebly whines the puddocks wail *kite's*
Slow circling naked woods around
And wild geese ranks that swifter sail
Oft start one with a hoarser sound
While towering at the farthest height
The heron brawls its lonley cry
Who interscepts the dazzld light
And looks a cloud speck in the skye 120

Composed 1820   First published 1935

THE LAST OF MARCH
written at Lolham Brigs

Though o'er the darksome northern hill
    Old ambush'd winter frowning flies,
And faintly drifts his threatening still
    In snowy sleet and blackening skies;
Yet where the willow leaning lies
    And shields beneath the budding flower,
Where banks to break the wind arise,
    Tis sweet to sit and spend an hour.

Though floods of winter bustling fall
  Adown the arches bleak and blea,   10
Though snow-storms clothe the mossy wall,
  And hourly whiten oer the lea,
Yet when from clouds the sun is free
  And warms the learning bird to sing
'Neath sloping bank and sheltering tree
  'Tis sweet to watch the creeping spring.

Though still so early, one may spy
  And track her footsteps every hour;
The daisy with its golden eye,
  And primrose bursting into flower;   20
And snugly where the thorny bower
  Keeps off the nipping frost and wind,
Excluding all but sun and shower,
  Their early violets children find.

Here 'neath the shelving bank's retreat
  The horse-blob swells its golden ball;
Nor fear the Lady-smocks to meet
  The snows that round their blossoms fall;
Here by the arches' ancient wall
  The antique Elder buds anew;   30
Again the bulrush sprouting tall
  The water wrinkles rippling through.

As Spring's warm herald April comes,
  As Natures sleep is nearly past,
How sweet to hear the wakening hums
  Of aught beside the Winter blast!
Of feather'd minstrels first and last
  The robins song's again begun
And as skies clear when overcast
  Larks rise to hail the peeping sun.   40

The startling pee-wits, as they pass,
  Scream joyous whizzing over head,

Right glad the fields and meadow grass
     Will quickly hide their careless shed:
The rooks where yonder <u>witchens</u> spread   *elms*
     Quawk clamorous to the spring's approach:
Here silent from its watery bed,
     To hail its coming, leaps the roach.

While stalking oer the fields again
     In stript defiance to the storms,   50
The hardy seedsman spreads the grain,
     And all his hopeful toil performs:
In flocks the timid pigeon swarms
     For scatter'd kernels chance may spare,
And as the plough unbeds the worms
     The crows and magpies gather there.

Yon bullocks low their liberty,
     The young grass cropping to the full;
And colts from straw-yards neighing free
     Spring's opening promise 'joy at will: 60
Along the bank, beside the rill
     The happy lambkins bleat and run,
Then weary, neath a sheltering hill
     Drop basking in the gleaming sun.

At distance from the water's edge,
     An hanging <u>sallows</u> farthest stretch,   *willow's*
The moor hen 'gins her nest of sedge
     Safe from destroying boys to reach.
Fen-sparrows chirp and fly to fetch
     The wither'd reed-down rustling nigh,   70
And by the sunny side the ditch
     Prepare their dwelling warm and dry.

Again a storm encroaches round,
     Thick clouds are darkening deep behind,
And through the arches hoarsely sound

The risings of the hollow wind:
Springs early hopes seem half resign'd,
   And silent for a while remain,
Till sunbeams broken clouds can find
   And brighten all to life again.   80

Ere yet a hailstone pattering comes,
   Or dimps the pool the rainy squall,
One hears the mighty murmuring hums,
   The Spirit of the tempest call.
Here sheltering 'neath the ancient wall
   I still pursue my musing dreams,
And as the hailstones round me fall
   I mark their bubbles in the streams.

Reflection here is warm'd to sigh,
   Tradition gives these brigs renown,   *bridges*   90
Though heedless Time long pass'd them by
   Nor thought them worthy noting down.
Here in the mouth of every clown
   The 'Roman road' familiar sounds;
All else with everlasting frown
   Oblivions mantling mist surrounds.

These walls the work of Roman hands!
   How may conjecturing Fancy pore,
As lonely here one calmly stands,
   On paths that age has trampled o'er.   100
The builders' names are known no more;
   No spot on earth their memory bears;
And crowds reflecting thus before
   Have since found graves as dark as their's.

The storm has ceas'd, – again the sun
   The ague-shivering season dries;
Short winded March, thou'lt soon be done,
   Thy fainting tempest mildly dies.

Soon April's flowers and dappled skies
   Shall spread a couch for lovely May,   110
Upon whose bosom Nature lies
   And smiles its' joyous Youth away.

Composed 1821   First published 1821

TO A FALLEN ELM

Old Elm that murmured in our chimney top
The sweetest anthem autumn ever made
And into mellow whispering calms would drop
When showers fell on thy many colored shade
And when dark tempests mimic thunder made
While darkness came as it would strangle light
With the black tempest of a winter night
That rocked thee like a cradle to thy root
How did I love to hear the winds upbraid
Thy strength without while all within was mute   10
It seasoned comfort to our hearts desire
We felt thy kind protection like a friend
And pitched our chairs up closer to the fire
Enjoying comforts that was never penned

Old favourite tree thoust seen times changes lower
But change till now did never come to thee
For time beheld thee as his sacred dower
And nature claimed thee her domestic tree
Storms came and shook thee with a living power
Yet stedfast to thy home thy roots hath been   20
Summers of thirst parched round thy homely bower
Till earth grew iron – still thy leaves was green
The children sought thee in thy summer shade
And made their play house rings of sticks and stone
The mavis sang and felt himself alone
While in thy leaves his early nest was made

84

And I did feel his happiness mine own
Nought heeding that our friendship was betrayed

Friend not inanimate — tho stocks and stones
There are and many cloathed in flesh and bones   30
Thou ownd a language by which hearts are stirred
Deeper than by the atribute of words
Thine spoke a feeling known in every tongue
Language of pity and the force of wrong
What cant asumes what hypocrites may dare
Speaks home to truth and shows it what they are

I see a picture that thy fate displays
And learn a lesson from thy destiny
Self interest saw thee stand in freedoms ways
So thy old shadow must a tyrant be   40
Thoust heard the knave abusing those in power
Bawl freedom loud and then oppress the free
Thoust sheltered hypocrites in many a shower
That when in power would never shelter thee
Thoust heard the knave supply his canting powers
With wrongs illusions when he wanted friends
That bawled for shelter when he lived in showers
And when clouds vanished made thy shade amends
With axe at root he felled thee to the ground
And barked of freedom — O I hate that sound   50

It grows the cant terms of enslaving tools
To wrong another by the name of right
It grows a liscence with oer bearing fools
To cheat plain honesty by force of might
Thus came enclosure — ruin was her guide
But freedoms clapping hands enjoyed the sight
Tho comforts cottage soon was thrust aside
And workhouse prisons raised upon the scite
Een natures dwelling far away from men
The common heath became the spoilers prey   60

85

The rabbit had not where to make his den
And labours only cow was drove away
No matter – wrong was right and right was wrong
And freedoms brawl was sanction to the song

Such was thy ruin music making Elm
The rights of freedom was to injure thine
As thou wert served so would they overwhelm
In freedoms name the little that is mine
And these are knaves that brawl for better laws
And cant of tyranny in stronger powers   70
Who glut their vile unsatiated maws
And freedoms birthright from the weak devours

Composed c. 1821   First published 1920

from A SUNDAY WITH
SHEPHERDS AND HERDBOYS

The shepherds and the herding swains
Keep their sabbath on the plains
They know no difference in its cares
Save that all toil has ceasd but theirs
For them the church bells vainly call
Fields are their church and house and all
Till night returns their homward track
When soon morns suns recall them back
Yet still they love the days repose
And feel its peace as sweet as those   10
That have their freedom – and maid and clown   ·laborer
To walk the meadows or the town
Theyll lye and catch the humming sound
That comes from steeples shining round
Enjoying in the service time
The happy bells delightfull chime
And oft they sit on rising ground

To view the landscap spreading round
Swimming from the following eye
In greens and stems of every dye   20
Oer wood and vale and fens smooth lap
Like a richly coulourd map
Square platts of clover red and white
Scented wi summers warm delight
And sinkfoil of a fresher stain   *cinquefoil*
And different greens of varied grain
Wheat spindles bursted into ear
And browning faintly – grasses sere
In swathy seed pods dryd by heat
Rustling when brushd by passing feet   30
And beans and peas of deadening green
And corn lands ribbon stripes between
And checkering villages that lye   *chessboard-like*
Like light spots in a deeper sky
And woods black greens that crowding spots
The lanscape in leaf bearing grots   *grottos*
Were mingling hid lapt up to lare
The panting fox lyes cooly there
And willow grove that idly sweas
And checkering shines mid other trees   40
As if the mornings misty vail
Yet lingerd in their shadows pale
While from the village foliage pops
The popples tapering to their tops   *poplars*
That in the blue sky thinly wires
Like so many leafy spires
Thus the shepherd as he lyes
Were the heaths furze swellings rise   *Where*
Dreams oer the scene in visions sweet
Stretching from his hawthorn seat   50
And passes many an hour away
Thus musing on the sabbath day
And from the fields theyll often steal
The green peas for a sunday meal

When near a farmers on the lurch   *never*
Safe nodding oer their books a church
Or on their benches by the door
Telling their market profits oer
And in snug nooks their huts beside
The gipsey blazes they provide   60
Braking the rotten from the trees
While some sit round to shell the peas
Or pick from hedges pilferd wood
To boil on props their stolen food
Sitting on stones or heaps of brakes   *bracken*
Each of the wild repast partakes
Telling to pass the hours along
Tales that to fitter days belong
While one within his scrip contains   *shepherds coat*
A shatterd bibles thumbd remains   70
On whose blank leaf wi pious care
A host of names is scribbld there
Names by whom twas once possest
Or those in kindred bonds carresst
Childern for generations back
That doubtful memory should not lack
Their dates tis there wi care applyd
When they were born and when they dyd
From sire to son link after link
All scribbld wi unsparing ink   80
This he will oft pull out and read
That takes of sunday better heed
Then they who laugh at tale and jest
And oft hell read it to the rest
Whose ignorance in weary mood
Pays more regard to robin hood
And giant blue beard and such tales
That live like flowers in rural vales
Natural as last years faded blooms
Anew wi the fresh season comes   90
So these old tales from old to young

Take root and blossom were they sprung
Till age and winter bids them wane
Then fond youth takes them up again
       [. . .]

Composed before 1826   *First published 1935*

from THE AUTOBIOGRAPHY

[. . .] I had plenty of leisure but it was the leisure of solitude
for my sundays were demanded to be spent in the fields at horse
or cow tending my whole summer was one days employment,
as it were in the fields I grew so much into the quiet love of
nature's perserves that I was never easy but when I was in the
fields passing my sabbaths and leisure with the shepherds &
herdboys as fancys prompted sometimes playing at marbles on
the smooth-beaten sheeptracks or leapfrog among the thymy
molehills sometimes running among the corn to get the red &
blue flowers for cockades to play at soldiers or running into the   10
woods to hunt strawberries or stealing peas in churchtime
when the owners were safe to boil at the gypsey's fire who went
half-shares at our stolen luxury we heard the bells chime but
the fields was our church & we seemd to feel a religious poetry
in our haunts on the sabbath while some old shepherd sat on a
molehill reading aloud some favourite chapter from an old
fragment of a Bible which he carried in his pocket for the day a
family relic which possesd on its covers & title pages in rude
scrawls genealogys of the third & fourth Generations when
aunts mothers & grandmothers dyd when cousins &c were   20
married & brothers & sisters born occupying all the blank
leaves in the book & the title pages which leaves were preservd
with a sacred veneration tho half the contents had been sufferd
to drop out & be lost.   boyhood
   I lovd this solitary disposition from a boy & felt a curiosity to
wander about spots were I had never been before I remember
one incident of this feeling when I was very young it cost my
parents some anxiety it was summer & I started off in the

89

morning to get rotten sticks from the woods but I had a feeling
to wander about the fields & I indulged it I had often seen the   30
large heath calld Emmonsales stretching its yellow furze from
my eye into unknown solitudes when I went with the mere
openers & my curiosity urgd me to steal an opportunity to
explore it that morning I had imagind that the world's end was
at the orizon & that a days journey was able to find it so I went
on with my heart full of hope's pleasures & discoverys expecting when I got to the brink of the world that I coud look down,
like looking into a large pit & see into its secrets the same as I
believd I coud see heaven by looking into the water So I eagerly
wanderd on & rambled along the furze the whole day till I got   40
out of my knowledge when the very wild flowers seemd to
forget me & I imagind they were the inhabitants of new
countrys the very sun seemd to be a new one & shining in a
different quarter of the sky still I felt no fear my wonder-seek-
ing happiness had no room for it I was finding new wonders
every minute & was walking in a new world & expecting the
world's end bye & bye but it never came often wondering to
myself that I had not found the edge of the old one the sky still
touchd the ground in the distance & my childish wisdom was
puzzld in perplexitys night came on before I had time to fancy   50
the morning was by which made me hasten to seek home I
knew not which way to turn but chance put me in the right
track & when I got back into my own fieldds I did not know
them everything lookd so different [. . .]

Composed 1824   First published 1951

MOORS
THE MORES   *(Enclosures)*

Far spread the moorey ground a level scene
Bespread with rush and one eternal green
That never felt the rage of blundering plough
Though centurys' wreathed springs blossoms on its brow
Still meeting plains that stretched them far away

In uncheckt shadows of green brown and grey
Unbounded freedom ruled the wandering scene
Nor fence of ownership crept in between
To hide the prospect of the following eye
Its only bondage was the circling sky   10
One mighty flat undwarfed by bush and tree
Spread its faint shadow of immensity
And lost itself which seemed to eke its bounds
In the blue mist the orisons edge surrounds   *horizon's*
Now this sweet vision of my boyish hours
Free as spring clouds and wild as summer flowers
Is faded all – a hope that blossomed free
And hath been once no more shall ever be
Inclosure came and trampled on the grave
Of labours rights and left the poor a slave   20
And memorys pride ere want to wealth did bow
Is both the shadow and the substance now
The sheep and cows were free to range as then
Where change might prompt nor felt the bonds of men
Cows went and came with evening morn and night
To the wild pasture as their common right
And sheep unfolded with the rising sun   *released from the fold*
Heard the swains shout and felt their freedom won
Tracked the red fallow field and heath and plain
Then met the brook and drank and roamed again   30
The brook that dribbled on as clear as glass
Beneath the roots they hid among the grass
While the glad shepherd traced their tracks along
Free as the lark and happy as her song
But now alls fled and flats of many a dye
That seemed to lengthen with the following eye
Moors loosing from the sight far smooth and blea
Where swopt the plover in its pleasure free
Are vanished now with commons wild and gay
As poets visions of lifes early day   40
Mulberry bushes where the boy would run
To fill his hands with fruit are grubbed and done

And hedgrow briars – flower lovers overjoyed
Came and got flower pots – these are all destroyed
And sky bound mores in mangled garbs are left
Like mighty giants of their limbs bereft
Fence now meets fence in owners little bounds
Of field and meadow large as garden grounds
In little parcels little minds to please
With men and flocks imprisoned ill at ease   50
Each little path that led its pleasant way
As sweet as morning leading night astray
Where little flowers bloomed round a varied host
That travel felt delighted to be lost   Traveler
Nor grudged the steps that he had taen as vain
When right roads traced his journeys end again
Nay on a broken tree hed sit awhile
To see the mores and fields and meadows smile
Sometimes with cowslaps smothered – then all white
With daiseys – then the summers splendid sight   60
Of corn fields crimson oer the 'headach' bloomd
Like splendid armys for the battle plumed
He gazed upon them with wild fancys eye
As fallen landscapes from an evening sky
These paths are stopt – the rude philistines thrall
Is laid upon them and destroyed them all
Each little tyrant with his little sign
Shows where man claims earth glows no more divine
On paths to freedom and to childhood dear
A board sticks up to notice 'no road here'   70
And on the tree with ivy overhung
The hated sign by vulgar taste is hung
As tho the very birds should learn to know
When they go there they must no further go
This with the poor scared freedom bade good bye
And much they feel it in the smothered sigh
And birds and trees and flowers without a name
All sighed when lawless laws enclosure came

And dreams of plunder in such rebel schemes
Have found too truly that they were but dreams   80

Composed 1821–4   First published 1935

THE LAMENT OF
SWORDY WELL

Petitioners are full of prayers
To fall in pity's way
But if her hand the gift forbears
Theyll sooner swear then pray   *than*
They're not the worst to want who lurch
On plenty with complaints
No more then those who go to church
Are eer the better saints

I hold no hat to beg a mite
Nor pick it up when thrown   10
Nor limping leg I hold in sight
But pray to keep my own
Where profit gets his clutches in
There's little he will leave
Gain stooping for a single pin
Will stick it on his sleeve

For passers bye I never pin
No troubles to my breast
Nor carry round some names
More money from the rest   20
Im swordy well a piece of land
That's fell upon the town
Who worked me till I couldnt stand
And crush me now Im down

93

In parish bonds I well may wail
Reduced to every shift
Pity may grieve at troubles tale
But cunning shares the gift
Harvests with plenty on his brow
Leaves losses taunts with me   30
Yet gain comes yearly with the plough
And will not let me be

Alas dependance thou'rt a brute
Want only understands
His feelings wither branch and root
That falls in parish hands
The muck that clouts the ploughmans shoe
The moss that hides the stone
Now Im become the parish due
Is more then I can own   40

Though Im no man yet any wrong
Some sort of right may seek
And I am glad if een a song
Gives me the room to speak
Ive got among such grubbling geer   grub-ax
And such a hungry pack
If I brought harvests twice a year
They'd bring me nothing back

When war their tyrant prices got
I trembled with alarms   50
They fell and saved my little spot
Or towns had turned to farms
Let profit keep an humble place
That gentry may be known
Let pedigrees their honours trace
And toil enjoy its own

The silver springs grown naked dykes
Scarce own a bunch of rushes

When grain got high the tasteless tykes
Grubbed up trees banks and bushes   60
And me they turned me inside out
For sand and grit and stones
And turned my old green hills about
And pickt my very bones

These things that claim my own as theirs
Where born but yesterday
But ere I fell to town affairs
I were as proud as they
I kept my horses cows and sheep
And built the town below   70
Ere they had cat or dog to keep
And then to use me so

Parish allowance gaunt and dread
Had it the earth to keep
Would even pine the bees to dead
To save an extra keep
Prides workhouse is a place that yields
From poverty its gains
And mines a workhouse for the fields
A starving the remains   80

The bees flye round in feeble rings
And find no blossom bye
Then thrum their almost weary wings
Upon the moss and die
Rabbits that find my hills turned oer
Forsake my poor abode
They dread a workhouse like the poor
And nibble on the road

If with a clover bottle now
Spring dares to lift her head   90
The next day brings the hasty plough

And makes me miserys bed
The butterflyes may wir and come
I cannot keep em now
Nor can they bear my parish home
That withers on my brow

No now not een a stone can lie
Im just what eer they like
My hedges like the winter flye
And leave me but the dyke   100
My gates are thrown from off the hooks
The parish thoroughfare
Lord he thats in the parish books
Has little wealth to spare

I couldnt keep a dust of grit
Nor scarce a grain of sand
But bags and carts claimed every bit
And now theyve got the land
I used to bring the summers life
To many a butterflye   110
But in oppressions iron strife
Dead tussocks bow and sigh

Ive scarce a nook to call my own
For things that creep or flye
The beetle hiding neath a stone
Does well to hurry bye
Stock eats my struggles every day
As bare as any road
He's sure to be in somthings way
If eer he stirs abroad   120

I am no man to whine and beg
But fond of freedom still
I hing no lies on pitys peg
To bring a gris to mill

On pitys back I neednt jump
My looks speak loud alone
My only tree they've left a stump
And nought remains my own

My mossy hills gains greedy hand
And more then greedy mind   130
Levels into a russet land
Nor leaves a bent behind
In summers gone I bloomed in pride
Folks came for miles to prize
My flowers that bloomed no where beside
And scarce believed their eyes

Yet worried with a greedy pack
They rend and delve and tear
The very grass from off my back
Ive scarce a rag to wear   140
Gain takes my freedom all away
Since its dull suit I wore
And yet scorn vows I never pay
And hurts me more and more

And should the price of grain get high
Lord help and keep it low
I shant possess a single flye
Or get a weed to grow
I shant possess a yard of ground
To bid a mouse to thrive   150
For gain has put me in a pound
I scarce can keep alive

I own Im poor like many more
But then the poor mun live   must
And many came for miles before
For what I had to give
But since I fell upon the town

They pass me with a sigh
I've scarce the room to say sit down
And so they wander bye 160

Though now I seem so full of clack
Yet when yer' riding bye
The very birds upon my back
Are not more fain to flye
I feel so lorn in this disgrace
God send the grain to fall
I am the oldest in the place
And the worst served of all

Lord bless ye I was kind to all
And poverty in me 170
Could always find a humble stall
A rest and lodging free
Poor bodys with an hungry ass
I welcomed many a day
And gave him tether room and grass
And never said him nay

There was a time my bit of ground
Made freemen of the slave
The ass no pindard dare to pound
When I his supper gave 180
The gipseys camp was not affraid
I made his dwelling free
Till vile enclosure came and made
A parish slave of me

The gipseys further on sojourn
No parish bounds they like
No sticks I own and would earth burn
I shouldnt own a dyke
I am no friend to lawless work
Nor would a rebel be 190

And why I call a christian turk
Is they are turks to me

And if I could but find a friend
With no deciet to sham
Who'd send me some few sheep to tend
And leave me as I am
To keep my hills from cart and plough
And strife of mongerel men
And as spring found me find me now
I should look up agen   200

And save his Lordships woods that past
The day of danger dwell
Of all the fields I am the last
That my own face can tell
Yet what with stone pits delving holes
And strife to buy and sell
My name will quickly be the whole
Thats left of swordy well

Composed 1821–4   First published 1935

from THE PROGRESS OF
RYHME

O soul enchanting poesy
Thoust long been all the world with me
When poor thy presence grows my wealth
When sick thy visions gives me health
When sad thy sunny smile is joy
And was from een a tiney boy
When trouble was and toiling care
Seemed almost more then I could bear
While thrashing in the dusty barn
Or squashing in the ditch to earn   10

A pittance that would scarce alow
One joy to smooth my sweating brow
Where drop by drop would chase and fall
– Thy presence triumphed over all
The vulgar they might frown and sneer
Insult was mean – but never near
T'was poesy's self that stopt the sigh
And malice met with no reply
So was it in my earlier day
When sheep to corn had strayed away   20
Or horses closen gaps had broke   *small Fields*
Ere sunrise peeped or I awoke
My master's frown might force the tear
But poesy came to check and cheer
It glistened in my shamed eye
But ere it fell the swoof was bye   *grief*
I thought of luck in future days
When even he might find a praise
I looked on poesy like a friend
To cheer me till my life should end   30
                    [. . .]

Composed 1821–4   First published 1908

from THE PARISH

'Prologue'

*'No injury can possibly be done, as a nameless character can never be found
out but by its truth and likeness'*

                                                    POPE

The Parish hind, oppression's humble slave,   *farm servant*
Whose only hopes of freedom is the grave
The cant miscalled religion in the saint

100

And Justice mockd while listning wants complaint
The parish laws and parish queens and kings
Prides lowest classes of pretending things
The meanest dregs of tyrany and crime
I fearless sing let truth attend the ryhme
Tho now adays truth grows a vile offence
And courage tells it at his own expence   10
If he but utter what himself has seen
He deals in satire and he wounds too keen
Intends sly ruin by encroached degrees
Is rogue or radical or what you please
But shoud vile flatterers with the basest lies
Attempt self interest with a wished disguise
Say groves of myrtle here in winter grow
And blasts blow blessings every time they blow
That golden showers in mercey fall to bless
The half thatchd mouldering hovels of distress   20
That edens self in freedoms infant sphere
Was but a desert to our Eden here
That laws so wise to choke the seeds of strife
Here bless a beggar with an Adams Life
Ah what an host of Patronizers then
Woud gather round the motley flatterers den
A spotted monster in a lambkins hide
Whose smooth tongue uttered what his heart denied
Theyd call his genius wonderous in extream
And lisp the novel beautys of his theme   30
And say twas luck on natures kinder part
To bless such genius with a gentle heart
Curst affectation worse then hell I hate
Thy sheepish features and thy crouching gait
Like sneeking cur that licks his masters shoe
Bowing and cringing to the Lord knows who
Licking the dust for each approving nod
Were pride is worshiped like an earthly god
The rogue thats carted to the gallows tree
Is far more honest in his trade then thee

there (left margin, line 38)
than (right margin, final line)

101

'Village patriots'

Young Brag a 'jack of all trades' save his own
From home is little as the farmer known   740
He talks with all the equal and the high
Equally ready to tell truth or lie
His betters view him in his just deserts
But equals deem him one of mighty parts
Opinions gratis gives in men's affairs
Fool in his own but wonderous wise in theirs
Upon his talents friends were strongly bent
Mistook his parts and off to school he went
A young aspiring hopeful youth at least
Whose parents deemd him fashiond for a priest   750
Twas somthing urgd the dissapointed view
With which religion had the least to do
Tho they baskd blessd in fortunes wealthy sun
They yearnd for more to bless their hopeful son
Whom school and colledge both had vainly taught
And learnd young hopeful to be fit for naught
His friends decievd beheld the faded charm
Resignd weak hopes and placed him in a farm
And there he lives and to great skill pretends
And reigns a god among his farming friends   760
Scrats paragraphs and sends them to the News   *scratches*
Signd 'constant reader' lest they shoud refuse
The illspelt trash on patriotic cavils
Leaving correction to the printers devils
Skits upon those by whom theyre never read
Who might as well write Letters to the dead
Or puffs upon himself in various ways
Whom none but self will either read or praise
And Poems too the polishd patriot chimes
Stanzas to Cobbets truth and Comic Ryhmes   770
To which he fits a hacknied tune that draws
From patriot dinners echoes of applause
And in the next weeks news out comes the treat

102   *William Cobbett, a leading
           radical journalist*

From 'constant reader' of the drunken feat

here Were so much wine is lavishd in the strain
As even to make the reader drunk again
Were every dish on which the knaves regale
Find places there but common sense and ale
For common sense is grown too tame to teach
And ales too low to aid a patriots speech   780
And morts of speeches made to back reform   *lots*
That raised applauses like a thunder storm
And almost loosd the rafters from their pegs
While chairs and tables scarce coud keep their legs
Reeling amid the hiccups and hurra's
And glass[es] rung and almost dancd applause
Nor will he pass his comic singing oer
For they too set the table in a roar
And then concludes it with the pompous clause
– Success to patriots and the good old cause   *parliamentary* 790
                                                  reform
A hacknied tune which patriots daily sing
Like variations of 'God save the King'
But when election mobs for battle meet
And dirty flags and ribbons throng the street
Hunting for votes some little borough town
Tis there his genius meets the most renown
When on the hustings bawling spouters throng
Who fight and war like women with the tongue
All speakers and no hearers were the crys   *where*
Piles up confusions babel to the skys   800
And croaking at the top in proud renown
Each party sits till tother pulls him down
Here shines our orator in all his plumes
Nor prouder bantum to a dung hill comes
han Then he to crow and peck and peck and crow
And hurl bad english at retorting foe

'The parish council'

Churchwardens Constables and Overseers   *poor-relief*
                                           officials   1220
Makes up the round of Commons and of Peers

With learning just enough to sign a name
And skill sufficient parish rates to frame
And cunning deep enough the poor to cheat
This learned body for debatings meet
Tho many heads the parliment prepare
And each one claims some wisdom for its share
Like midnight with her vapours tis so small
They make but darkness visible withall
Their secretary is the Parish Clerk   1230
Whom like a shepherds dog they keep to bark
And gather rates and when the next are due
To cry them òer at church time from his pew
He as their 'Jack of all trades' steady shines
Thro thick and thin to sanction their designs
Who apes the part of King and Magistrate
And acts grand segnior of this turkish state
Who votes new laws to those already made
And acts by force when one is disobeyd
Having no credit which he fears to loose   1240
He does what ever dirty jobs they chuse
Knight of the black staff master of the stocks
And hand cuff keeper – tools that sadly mock
His dignity – for common sense will sneer
And half acknowledge in his passing ear
That such like tools and titles near was known   *never*
To grace a name so aptly as his own
For though with natural cunning fortified
His deeds will often grow too large to hide
Tho' like a smugglers dealings shunning light   1250
They peep thro' rents and often sprout in sight
Thus summons oft are served in hopes of pelf
To overcharge and get a fee for self
And village dances watched at midnight hours
In the mock errand of his ruleing powers
With feigned pretence good order to preserve
Only to break it if a chance shoud serve
For married clowns his actions closely mark

104   *laborers*

And jealous grow at whispers in the dark
Whence broils ensue – then from the noisey fray 1260
Himself hath made sneaks unpercieved away
Like to the fox whom yard dogs' barks affright
When on the point of robbing roosts at night
Such is this Sancho of the magistrates *Sancho Panza, i, e.,*
And such are most knaves of those petty states *servant*
Where cunning fools are only reckoned wise
Who best can hide their faults from others' eyes
And bold assurance forging merits' place
Takes credit to be bad were all are base *where*
Whose Staff becomes his law and succour too 1270
The stoutest village rabble to subdue
Soon as he holds it in his mighty hand
It grows as potent as a magic wand
Clowns look and grow submissive at the view
As if the mighty weapon froze them thro
For when a Hudibrass oersteps the laws *comic characters*
A Ralph is ready to defend his cause
Tasking the pauper [his] labours to stand
Or clapping on his goods the Parish Brand
Lest he shoud sell them for the want of bread 1280
On parish bounty rather pind then fed *pined, than*
Or carrying the parish book from door to door
Claiming fresh taxes from the needy poor
And if ones hunger overcomes his hate
And buys a loaf with what shoud pay the rate
He instant sets his tyrant laws to work
In heart and deed the essence of a turk
Brings summons for an eighteen penny rate
And gains the praises of the parish state
Or seizes goods and from the burthend clown 1290
Extorts for extra trouble half a Crown
Himself a beggar that may shortly take
A weekly pittance from the rates they make
But the old proverb suits the subject well
Mount such on horseback and they'll ride to hell

105

Such is this fussy cur that well deserves
The business of the master whom he serves
The vilest thing neer crawled without its brother
And theyre as like as one Ass gets another
One sets no job but tother barks to do't   1300
Both for self interest lick the foulest foot
And spite of all the meaness and the stink
Picks up gains crumbles from the dirtiest sink   *crumbs*
One name serves both and that I need not name
For all may by the color know the game
As hungry dogs know carrion by the smell
So all may know them by their ways as well
Coarse as such images but nought would do
But coarsest stuff to make the picture true
As when some muse weeps over Tyburn tree   *the gallows* 1310
Hard words and hanging make the melody
So as they reign here let them hang together
Stinking when met like sinks in stormy weather
Tho natures marks are deep that all may scan
A knaves delusions from an honest man
Oppression often mourns the vile abuse
And flyes to justice – deemd of little use
Truth that coud once its own redresses seek
Is now deemd nothing and forbid to speak
Driven like an exild king from past renown   1320
Power took its place and keeps it with a frown
But tis well known that justice winks at crimes
A saying thats in season at all times
Or why should the poor sinning starving clown
Meet jail and hanging for a stolen crown
While wealthy thieves with knaverys bribes endued
Plunder their millions and are not pursued
Nay at the foot of Tyburns noted tree
They do deserving deeds and still go free
Where others suffer for some pigmy cause   1330
They all but murder and escape the laws
Skulking awhile in briberys dirty den

106

Then start new gilt and pass as honest men
And why shoud power or pride betray its trust?
Is it too old a fashion to be just
Or does self-interest inclinations bend?
Aye Aye the Farmer is his worships friend
As parish priest from him he meets his tythes
Punctual as harvest wakes the tinkling sythes
Tho often grudgd yet he their hopes to glad   1340
Prays better harvests when the last was bad
And as he deals so honestly with him
It must be malice in the poor or whim
Who seek relief and lay on them the blame
And hopless seek it and return the same
Within the church where they on sabbath days
Mock god with all the outward show of praise
Making his house a pharisees at best
Gods for one day and Satans all the rest
The parson oft scarce puts his sermon bye   1350
Ere neath his pulpit and with mighty cry
The clerk announces – what? – commandments meet?
No – when these parish vestrys next shall meet
To fleece the poor and rob with vile command
Want of its bread too feeble to withstand   The needy
Altho its aching heart too often knows
Knaves call it debtor where it nothing owes
For in these Vestrys cunning deep as night
Plans deeds that would be treason to the light
And tho so honest in its own disguise   1360
Twould be plain theft exposed to reasons eyes
For the whole set just as they please can plan
And what one says all sanction to a man
Self interest rules each vestry they may call
And what one sticks for is the gain of all
The set – thus knavery like contagion runs
And thus the fathers card becomes the sons
Both play one game to cheat us in the lump
And the sons turn-up shows the fathers trump

107

'The workhouse'

Shoved as a nusiance from prides scornfull sight
In a cold corner stands in wofull plight
The shatterd workhouse of the parish poor   1790
And towards the north wind opes the creaking door
A makeshift shed for misery – no thought
Urgd plans for comfort when the work was wrought
No garden spot was left dull want to cheer
And make the calls for hunger less severe
With wholsome herbs that summers might supply
Twas not contrived for want to live but dye   *the needy*
A forced consern to satisfy the law   *concern*
Built want this covering oer his bed of straw
Een that cheap blessing thats so freely given   1800
To all that liveth neath the face of heaven
The light of day is not alowd to win
A smiling passage to the glooms within
No window opens on the southern sky
A luxury deemd to prides disdainful eye
The scant dull light that forcefull need supplyd
Scorn frownd and placed them on the sunless side
Here dwell the wretched lost to hopless strife
Reduced by want to skelletons in life
Despised by all een age grown bald and grey   1810
Meets scoffs from wanton childern in their play
Who laugh at misery by misfortune bred
And points scorns finger at the mouldering shed
The tottering tennant urges no replye
Turns his white head and chokes the passing sigh
And seeks his shed and hides his hearts despair
For pity lives not as a listner there
When no one hears or heeds he wakes to weep
On his straw bed as hunger breaks his sleep
And thinks oer all his troubles and distress   1820
With not one hope that life shall make them less
Save silent prayers that every woe may have

A speedy ransom in the peaceful grave
Close-fisted justice tho his only friend
Doth but cold comforts to his miserys lend
For six days only it alows its fee
Pay scarce sufficient for the wants of three
And for the seventh which god sent to rest
The weary limbs of labouring man and beast
He too may pay for what blind justice cares   1830
They've nought for sunday but the parsons prayers

Composed 1820–4   First published 1935

TO THE SNIPE

Lover of swamps
The quagmire overgrown
With hassock tufts of sedge – where fear encamps
Around thy home alone

The trembling grass
Quakes from the human foot
Nor bears the weight of man to let him pass
Where he alone and mute

Sitteth at rest
In safety 'neath the clump   10
Of hugh flag-forrest that thy haunts invest
Or some old sallow stump

Thriving on seams
That tiney islands swell
Just hilling from the mud and rancid streams
Suiting thy nature well

For here thy bill
Suited by wisdom good
Of rude unseemly length doth delve and drill
The gelid mass for food   20

109

And here may hap
When summer suns hath drest
The moor's rude desolate and spungy lap
May hide thy mystic nest

Mystic indeed
For isles that ocean make
Are scarcely more secure for birds to build
Then this flag-hidden lake

Boys thread the woods
To their remotest shades   30
But in these marshy flats these stagnant floods
Security pervades

From year to year
Places untrodden lye
Where man nor boy nor stock hath ventured near
– Nought gazed on but the sky

And fowl that dread
The very breath of man
Hiding in spots that never knew his tread
A wild and timid clan   40

Wigeon and teal
And wild duck – restless lot
That from man's dreaded sight will ever steal
To the most dreary spot

Here tempests howl
Around each flaggy plot
Where they who dread man's sight the water fowl
Hide and are frighted not

Tis power divine
That heartens them to brave   50

110

The roughest tempest and at ease recline
On marshes or the wave

Yet instinct knows
Not safety's bounds to shun
The firmer ground where skulking fowler goes
With searching dogs and gun

By tepid springs
Scarcely one stride across
Though brambles from its edge a shelter flings
Thy safety is at loss   60

And never chuse
The little sinky foss
Streaking the moores whence spa-red water spews
From puddles fringed with moss

Free booters there
Intent to kill and slay
Startle with cracking guns the trepid air
And dogs thy haunts betray

From dangers reach
Here thou art safe to roam   70
Far as these washy flag-worn marshes stretch
A still and quiet home

In these thy haunts
I've gleaned habitual love
From the vague world where pride and folly taunts
I muse and look above

Thy solitudes
The unbounded heaven esteems
And here my heart warms into higher moods
And dignifying dreams   80

111

I see the sky
Smile on the meanest spot
Giving to all that creep or walk or flye
A calm and cordial lot

Thine teaches me
Right feelings to employ
That in the dreariest places peace will be
A dweller and a joy

Composed 1821–4   First published 1935

THE WOODMAN

Now evening comes and from the new laid hedge
The woodman rustles in his leathern guise
Hiding in dyke ylined with brustling sedge
His <u>bill</u> and mittens from theft's meddling eyes   *pruning-hook*
And in his wallets storing many a pledge
Of flowers and boughs from early sprouting trees
And painted <u>pootys</u> from the ivied hedge   *snail shells*
About its mossy roots – his boys to please
Who wait with merry joy his coming home
Anticipating presents such as these   10
Gained far afield where they nor night nor morn
Find no school leisure long enough to go
Where flowers but rarely from their stalks are torn
And birds scarce loose a nest the season through

Composed 1821–4   First published 1835

THE COTTAGER

True as the church clock hand the hour pursues
He plods about his toils and reads the news
And at the blacksmith's shop his hour will stand
To talk of '<u>Lunun</u>' as a foreign land   *London*

112

For from his cottage door in peace or strife
He neer went fifty miles in all his life
His knowledge with old notions still combined
Is fifty years behind the march of mind
He views new knowledge with suspicious eyes
And thinks it blasphemy to be so wise   10
Oer steams almighty tales he wondering looks   *steam engines*
As witchcraft gleaned from old black letter books
Life gave him comfort but denied him wealth
He toils in quiet and enjoys his health
He smokes a pipe at night and drinks his beer
And runs no scores on tavern screens to clear
He goes to market all the year about
And keeps one hour and never stays it out
Een at St Thomas tide old Rovers bark   *Dec. 21*
Hails Dapples trot an hour before its dark   20
He is a simple-worded plain old man
Whose good intents take errors in their plan
Oft sentimental and with saddend vein
He looks on trifles and bemoans their pain
And thinks the angler mad and loudly storms
With emphasis of speech oer murdered worms
And hunters cruel – pleading with sad care
Pitys petition for the fox and hare
Yet feels self-satisfaction in his woes
For wars crushed myriads of his slaughtered foes   30
He is right scruplous in one pretext
And wholesale errors swallows in the next
He deems it sin to sing yet not to say
A song a mighty difference in his way
And many a moving tale in antique ryhmes
He has for christmass and such merry times
When chevey chase his master piece of song   *an old ballad*
Is said so earnest none can think it long
Twas the old Vicars way who should be right
For the late Vicar was his hearts delight   40
And while at church he often shakes his head

113

To think what sermons the old Vicar made
Down right and orthodox that all the land
Who had their ears to hear might understand
But now such mighty learning meets his ears
He thinks it greek or lattin which he hears
Yet church recieves him every sabbath day
And rain or snow he never keeps away
All words of reverence still his heart reveres
Low bows his head when Jesus meets his ears   50
And still he thinks it blasphemy as well
Such names without a capital to spell
In an old corner cupboard by the wall
His books are laid – tho good in number small
His Bible first in place – from worth and age
Whose grandsires name adorns the title page
And blank leaves once now filled with kindred claims
Display a worlds epitome of names
Parents and childern and grandchildern – all
Memorys affections in the list recall   60
And Prayer book next much worn tho strongly bound
Proves him a churchman orthodox and sound
The 'Pilgrims Progress' too and 'Death of Abel'
Are seldom missing from his sunday table
And prime old Tusser in his homely trim   *author of a book*
The first of Bards in all the world with him *on husbandry*
And only poet which his leisure knows
– Verse deals in fancy so he sticks to prose
These are the books he reads and reads again
And weekly hunts the almanacks for rain   70
Here and no further learnings channels ran
Still neighbours prize him as the learned man
His cottage is a humble place of rest
With one spare room to welcome every guest
And that tall poplar pointing to the sky
His own hand planted when an idle boy
It shades his chimney while the singing wind
Hums songs of shelter to his happy mind

Within his cot the 'largest ears of corn'
He ever found his picture frames adorn   80
Brave Granby's Head – De Grasse's grand defeat   *English battles*
He rubs his hands and tells how Rodney beat
And from the rafters upon strings depend
Bean stalks beset with pods from end to end
Whose numbers without counting may be seen
Wrote on the Almanack behind the screen
Around the corner upon worsted strung
Pootys in wreaths above the cupboards hung   *snail shells*
Memory at trifling incidents awakes
And there he keeps them for his childern's sakes   90
Who when as boys searched every sedgy lane
Traced every wood and shattered cloaths again
Roaming about on raptures easy wing
To hunt those very Pooty shells in spring
And thus he lives too happy to be poor
While strife neer pauses at so mean a door
Low in the sheltered valley stands his cot
He hears the mountain storm and feels it not
Winter and spring toil ceasing ere tis dark
Rests with the lamb and rises with the lark   100
Content is helpmate to the day's employ
And care neer comes to steal a single joy
Time scarcely noticed turns his hair to grey
Yet leaves him happy as a child at play

Composed 1821–4   First published 1908

from THE SHEPHERD'S CALENDAR

from *'June'*

The shepherds idle hours are over now
Nor longer leaves him neath the hedgrow bough
On shadow pillowd banks and lolling stile
Wilds looses now their summer friends awhile

115

See also 'February', in The New Oxford Book of English Verse.

Shrill whistles barking dogs and chiding scold
Drive bleating sheep each morn from fallow fold   60
To wash pits were the willow shadows lean   *where*
Dashing them in their fold staind coats to clean
Then turnd on sunning sward to dry agen
They drove them homeward to the clipping pen
In hurdles pent were elm or sycamore
Shut out the sun – or in some threshing floor
There they wi scraps of songs and laugh and [t]ale
Lighten their anual toils while merry ale
Goes round and gladdens old mens' hearts to praise
The thread bare customs of old farmers' days   70
Who while the shrinking sheep wi trembling fears
Lies neath the snipping of his harmless sheers
Recalls full many a thing by bards unsung
And pride forgot – that reignd when he was young
How the hugh bowl was in the middle set
At breakfast time as clippers yearly met
Filld full of frumity were yearly swum   *a drink*
The streaking sugar and the spotting plumb
Which maids coud never to the table bring
Without one rising from the merry ring   80
To lend a hand who if twas taen amiss
Woud sell his kindness for a stolen kiss
The large stone pitcher in its homly trim
And clouded pint horn wi its copper rim   *drinking vessil*
Oer which rude healths was drank in spirits high
From the best broach the cellar woud supply
While sung the ancient swains in homly ryhmes
Songs that were pictures of the good old times
When leathern bottles held the beer nut brown
That wakd the sun wi songs and sung him down   90
Thus will the old man ancient ways bewail
Till toiling sheers gain ground upon the tale
And brakes it off – when from the timid sheep
The fleece is shorn and wi a fearfull leap
He starts – while wi a pressing hand

116

His sides are printed by the tarry brand
Shaking his naked skin wi wondering joys
And fresh ones are tugd in by sturdy boys
Who when they're thrown down 'neath the sheering swain
Will wipe his brow and start his tale again   100
Tho fashions haughty frown hath thrown aside
Half the old forms simplicity supplyd
Yet their are some prides winter deigns to spare
Left like green ivy when the trees are bare
And now when sheering of the flocks are done
Some ancient customs mixd wi harmless fun
Crowns the swains merry toils – the timid maid
Pleasd to be praisd and yet of praise affraid
Seeks her best flowers not those of woods and fields
But such as every farmers garden yields   110
Fine cabbage roses painted like her face
And shining pansys trimmd in golden lace
And tall tuft larkheels featherd thick wi flowers
And woodbines climbing oer the door in bowers
And London tufts of many a mottld hue
And pale pink pea and monkshood darkly blue
And white and purple jiliflowers that stay
Lingering in blossom summer half away
And single blood walls of a lucious smell
Old fashion flowers which huswives love so well   120
And columbines stone blue or deep night brown
Their honey-comb-like blossoms hanging down
Each cottage gardens fond adopted child
Tho heaths still claim them <u>were</u> they yet grow wild   *where*
Mong their old wild companions summer blooms
Furze brake and <u>mozzling</u> ling and golden broom   *mottled*
Snap dragons gaping like to sleeping clowns
And 'clipping pinks' (which maidens sunday gowns
Full often wear catcht at by <u>tozing</u> chaps)   *snatching*
Pink as the ribbons round their snowy caps   130
'Bess in her bravery' too of glowing dyes
As deep as sunsets crimson pillowd skyes

117

And marjoram notts sweet briar and ribbon grass
And lavender the choice of every lass
And sprigs of lads love all familiar names
Which every garden thro the village claims
These the maid gathers wi a coy delight
And tyes them up in readiness for night
Giving to every swain 'tween love and shame
Her 'clipping poseys' as their yearly claim   140
And turning as he claims the custom kiss
Wi stifld smiles half ankering after bliss   *hankering*
She shrinks away and blushing calls it rude
But turns to smile and hopes to be pursued
While one to whom the seeming hint applied
Follows to claim it and is not denyd
No doubt a lover for within his coat
His nosgay owns each flower of better sort
And when the envious mutter oer their beer
And nodd the secret to his neighbor near   150
Raising the laugh to make the mutter known
She blushes silent and will not disown
And ale and songs and healths and merry ways
Keeps up a shadow of old farmers' days
But the old beachen bowl that once supplyd
Its feast of frumity is thrown aside
And the old freedom that was living then
When masters made them merry wi their men
Whose coat was like his neighbors russet brown
And whose rude speech was vulgar as his clown   *laborer*   160
Who in the same horn drank the rest among
And joind the chorus while a labourer sung
All this is past – and soon may pass away
The time-torn remnant of the holiday
As proud distinction makes a wider space
Between the genteel and the vulgar race
Then must they fade as pride oer custom showers
Its blighting mildew on her feeble flowers

November

The village sleeps in mist from morn till noon
And if the sun wades thro tis wi a face
Beamless and pale and round as if the moon
When done the journey of its nightly race
Had found him sleeping and supplyd his place
For days the shepherds in the fields may be
Nor mark a patch of sky – blindfold they trace
The plains that seem wi out a bush or tree
Wistling aloud by guess to flocks they cannot see

The timid hare seems half its fears to loose   10
Crouching and sleeping neath its grassy lare
And scarcly startles tho the shepherd goes
Close by its home and dogs are barking there
The wild colt only turns around to stare
At passers bye then naps his hide again
And moody crows beside the road forbear
To flye tho pelted by the passing swain
Thus day seems turned to night and trys to wake in vain

The Owlet leaves her hiding place at noon
And flaps her grey wings in the doubting light   20
The hoarse jay screams to see her out so soon
And small birds chirp and startle with affright
Much doth it scare the superstitious wight
Who dreams of sorry luck and sore dismay
While cow boys think the day a dream of night
And oft grow fearful on their lonly way
Who fancy ghosts may wake and leave their graves by day

The cleanly maiden thro the village streets
In pattens clicks down causways never drye
While eves above head drops – were oft she meets   *where*   30
The schoolboy leering on wi mischiefs eye
Trying to splash her as he hurrys bye

119

While swains afield returning to their ploughs
Their passing aid wi gentle speech apply
And much loves rapture thrills when she alows
Their help wi offerd hand to lead her oer the sloughs

The hedger soakd wi the dull weather chops
On at his toils which scarcly keeps him warm
And every stroke he takes large swarms of drops
Patter about him like an april storm   40
The sticking dame wi cloak upon her arm
To guard against a storm walks the wet leas
Of willow groves or hedges round the farm
Picking up aught her splashy wanderings sees
Dead sticks the sudden winds have shook from off the trees

The boy that scareth from the spirey wheat
The mellancholy crow – quakes while he weaves
Beneath the ivey tree a hut and seat
Of rustling flags and sedges tyd in sheaves
Or from nigh stubble shocks a shelter thieves   50
There he doth dithering sit or entertain
His leisure hours down hedges lost to leaves
While spying nests where he spring eggs hath taen
He wishes in his heart twas summer time again

And oft he'll clamber up a sweeing tree   s w i n g i n g
To see the scarlet hunter hurry bye
And feign woud in their merry uproar be
But sullen labour hath its tethering tye
Crows swop around and some on bushes nigh   s w o o p
Watch for a chance when ere he turns away   60
To settle down their hunger to supply
From morn to eve his toil demands his stay
Save now and then an hour which leisure steals for play

Gaunt greyhounds now their coursing sports impart
Wi long legs stretchd on tip toe for the chase

120

And short loose ear and eye upon the start
Swift as the wind their motions they unlace
When bobs the hare up from her hiding place
Who in its furry coat of <u>fallow stain</u>   *pale brown*
Squats on the lands or wi a dodging pace   70
Tryes its old coverts of wood grass to gain
And oft by cunning ways makes all their speed in vain

Dull for a time the slumbering weather flings
Its murky prison round then winds wake loud
Wi sudden start the once still forest sings
Winters returning song cloud races cloud
And the orison throws away its shrowd
And sweeps its stretching circle from the eye
Storm upon storm in quick succession crowd
And oer the sameness of the purple skye   80
Heaven paints its wild irregularity

The shepherd oft foretells by simple ways
The weathers change that will ere long prevail
He marks the dull ass that grows wild and brays
And sees the old cows gad adown the vale
A summer race and snuff the coming gale
The old dame sees her cat wi fears alarm
Play hurly burly races wi its tale
And while she stops her wheel her hands to warm
She rubs her shooting corns and prophecys a storm   90

<u>Morts</u> are the signs – the stone-hid toad will croak   *Many*
And gobbling turkey cock wi noises vile
Dropping his snout as flaming as a cloak
Loose as a red rag oer his beak the while
Urging the dame to turn her round and smile
To see his uncooth pride her <u>cloaths</u> attack   *clothes*
Sidling wi wings hung down in vapoury broil
And feathers ruffld up while oer his back
His tail spreads like a fan cross wavd wi bars of black

121

The hog sturts round the stye and champs the straw   100
And bolts about as if a dog was bye
The steer will cease its gulping cud to chew
And toss his head wi wild and startld eye
At windshook straws – the geese will noise and flye
Like wild ones to the pond – wi matted mane
The cart horse squeals and kicks his partner nigh
While leaning oer his fork the foddering swain
The uproar marks around and dreams of wind and rain

And quick it comes among the forest oaks
Wi sobbing ebbs and uproar gathering high   110
The scard hoarse raven on its cradle croaks
And stock dove flocks in startld terrors flye
While the blue hawk hangs oer them in the skye
The shepherd happy when the day is done
Hastes to his evening fire his cloaths to dry
And forrester crouchd down the storm to shun
Scarce hears amid the strife the poacher's muttering gun

The ploughman hears the sudden storm begin
And hies for shelter from his naked toil
Buttoning his doublet closer to his chin   120
He speeds him hasty oer the elting soil   *damp*
White clouds above him in wild fury boil
And winds drive heavily the beating rain
He turns his back to catch his breath awhile
Then ekes his speed and faces it again   *increases*
To seek the shepherds hut beside the rushy plain

Oft stripping cottages and barns of thack   *thatch*
Were startld farmer garnerd up his grain   *where*
And wheat and bean and oat and barley stack
Leaving them open to the beating rain   130
The husbandman grieves oer his loss in vain
And sparrows mourn their night nests spoild and bare
The thackers they resume their toils again   *thatchers*

And stubbornly the tall red ladders bare
While to oerweight the wind they hang old harrows there

Thus wears the month along in checkerd moods
Sunshine and shadow tempest loud and calms
One hour dyes silent oer the sleepy woods
The next wakes loud with unexpected storms
A dreary nakedness the field deforms   140
Yet many rural sounds and rural sights
Live in the village still about the farms
Where toils rude uproar hums from morn till night
Noises in which the ear of industry delights

Hoarse noise of field-free bull that strides ahead
Of the tail switching herd to feed again
The barking mastiff from his kennel bed
Urging his teazing noise at passing swain
The jostling rumble of the starting wain   *wagon*
From the farm yard were freedoms chance to wait   150
The turkey drops his snout and geese in vain
Noise at the signal of the opening gate
Then from the clowns whip flyes and finds the chance too   *laborer's*
    late

The pigeon wi its breast of many hues
That spangles to the sun turns round and round
About his timid sidling mate and croos
Upon the cottage ridge were oer their heads   *where*
The puddock sails oft swopping oer the pen   *kite (hawk)*
Were timid chickens from their parent stray
That skulk and scutter neath her wings agen   160
Nor peeps no more till they have saild away

Such rural sounds the mornings tongue renews
And rural sights swarm on the rustics eye
The billy goat shakes from his beard the dews
And jumps the wall wi country teams to hie

Upon the barn rig at their freedom flye
The spotted guiney fowl – hogs in the stye
Agen the door in rooting whinings stand
The freed colt drops his head and gallops bye
The boy that holds a scuttle in his hand   170
Prefering unto toil the commons rushy land

At length the busy noise of toil is still
And industry awhile her care forgoes
When winter comes in earnest to fulfill
Her yearly task at bleak november's close
And stops the plough and hides the field in snows
When frost locks up the streams in chill delay
And mellows on the hedge the purple <u>sloes</u>   *berries*
For little birds – then toil hath time for play
And nought but threshers' flails awake the dreary day   180

Composed 1823–4   First published 1827

from CHILDHOOD

Each noise that breathed around us then
Was magic all and song
Where ever pastime found us then
Joy never led us wrong   180
The wild bee in the blossom hung
The coy birds startled call
To find its home in danger – there
Was music in them all

And oer the first <u>Bumbarrels'</u> nest   *a small bird*
We wondered at the spell
That birds who served no prenticeship
Could build their nests so well
And finding linnets' moss was green
And buntings chusing grey   190

And every buntings nest alike
Our wits was all away

Then blackbirds lining them with grass
And thrushes theirs with dung
So for our lives we could not tell
From whence the wisdom sprung
We marvelled much how little birds
Should ever be so wise
And so we guessed some angel came
To teach them from the skys   200

In winter too we traced the fields
And still felt summer joys
We sought our hips and felt no cold
Cold never came to boys
The sloes appeared as choice as plumbs
When bitten by the frost
And crabs grew honey in the mouth
When apple time was past

We rolled in sunshine lumps of snow
And called them mighty men   210
And tired of pelting Bounaparte
We ran to slide agen
And ponds for glibbest ice we sought   *smoothest*
With shouting and delight
And tasks of spelling all were left
To get by heart at night

And when it came – and round the fire
We sat – what joy was there
The kitten dancing round the cork
That dangled from a chair   220
While we our scraps of paper burnt
To watch the flitting sparks
And collect books were often torn
For 'parsons' and for 'clerks'

Nought seemed too hard for us to do
But the sums upon our slates
Nought seemed too high for us to win
But the master's chair of state
The 'Town of Troy' we tried and made
When our sums we could not trye   230
While we envied een the sparrows wings
From our prison house to flye

When twelve oclock was counted out
The joy and strife began
The shut of books the hearty shout
As out of doors we ran
Sunshine and showers who could withstand
Our food and rapture they
We took our dinners in our hands
To loose no time in play   240

The morn when first we went to school
Who can forget the morn
When the birch whip lay upon the clock
And our horn book it was torn
We tore the little pictures out
Less fond of books then play   than
And only took one letter home
And that the letter 'A'

I love in childhood's little book
To read its lessons thro   250
And oer each pictured page to look
Because they read so true
And there my heart creates anew
Love for each trifling thing
– Who can disdain the meanest weed
That shows its face at spring

The daisey looks up in my face
As long ago it smiled

126

It knows no change but keeps its place
And takes me for a child   260
The bunting in the hedgerow thorn
Cries 'pink pink pink' to hear
My footsteps in the early morn
As tho a boy was near

I seek no more the buntings nest
Nor stoop for daisey flowers
I grow a stranger to myself
In these delightful hours
Yet when I hear the voice of spring
I can but call to mind   270
The pleasures which they used to bring
The joys I used to find

The firetail on the orchard wall
Keeps at its startled cry
Of 'tweet tut tut' nor sees the morn
Of boyhoods mischief bye
It knows no change of changing time
By sickness never stung
It feeds on hopes eternal prime
Around its brooded young   280

Ponds where we played at 'Duck and drake'
Where the Ash with ivy grew
Where we robbed the owl of all her eggs
And mocked her as she flew
The broad tree in the spinney hedge
Neath which the gipseys lay
Where we our fine oak apples got
On the twenty ninth of may

These all remain as then they were
And are not changed a day   290
And the ivys crowns as near to green

As mine is to the grey
It shades the pond oerhangs the stile
And the oak is in the glen
But the paths to joy are so worn out
I cant find one agen

Composed 1824–32   First published 1935

'MEMORIES OF CHILDHOOD'

[. . .] I usd to be very fond of fishing & of a Sunday morning I
have been out before the sun delving for worms on some old
weed-blanketed dunghill & sliving off across the wet grass that
overhung the narrow path then,I usd to stop to wring my wet
trouser-bottoms now & then & off agen,beating the heavy
drops off the grass with my pole-end till I came to the flood-
washd meadow stream,my tackle was eagerly fastened on & my
heart woud thrill with hopes of success as I saw a sizable
gudgeon twinkle round the glossy pebbles or a fish leap after a
flye or a floating something on the deeper water,where is the   10
angler that hath not felt these delights in his young days &
where is the angler that doth not feel taken with their memory
when he is old ?

I usd also to be very fond of poking about the hedges in
spring to hunt pootys & I was no less fond of robbing the poor
birds nests or searching among the prickly furze on the heath,
poking sticks into the rabbit holes & carefully observing when
I took it out if there was down on the end which was a sign of a
nest with young then in went the arm up to the shoulder; &
then fear came upon us that a snake might be concealed in the   20
hole,our bloods ran cold within us & started us off to other
sports,we usd to chase the squirrels in the woods from grain to
grain that would sit washing their faces on the other side &
then peep at us again,we usd to get boughs from the trees, to
beat a wasps nest till some of us were stung & then we ran
away to other amusements

& then the year usd to be crownd with its holidays as thick as the boughs on a harvest-home, there was the long-wishd-for Christmas the celebrated week with two Sundays when we usd to watch the clerk return with his bundle of evergreens & run 30 for our bunch to stick [in] the windows & empty candlesticks hanging in the corner or hasten to the woods to get ivy branches with their jocolat berries which our parents usd to color with whiting & the blue-bag sticking the branches behind the pictures on the walls.

Then came valentine, though young we were not without loves, we had our favourites in the village & we listend the expected noises of creeping feet & the tinkling latch as eagerly as upgrown loves, wether they came or not it made no matter, dissapointment was nothing in those matters then, the pleasure 40 was all, then came the first of April, O how we talked & hoiped of it ere it came of how we woud make April fool of others & take care not to be caught ourselves when as soon as the day came we were the first to be taken in by running on errands for pigeon's milk & glass-eyed needles or some such April fool, when we were undeceivd we blushd for shame & took care not to be taken in again till the day returned when the old deceptions were so far forgotten as to deceive us again

Then there was the first of May, we were too young to be claimants in the upgrown sports but we joind our little interfer- 50 ences with them & ran under the extended handkerchiefs with the rest unmolested, then came the feast when the Cross was throngd round with stalls of toys & many colord sugar-plums & sweets horses on wheels with their flowing manes lambs with their red necklaces & box-cuckoos, we lookd on these fineries till the imagination almost coaxd our itching fingers to steal & seemd to upbraid our fears for not daring to do it, the sweetmeats were unbounded, there was barley-sugar candied lemon candied horehound & candied peppermint with swarms of colord sugar-plums & tins of lollypops, our mouths watered 60 at such luxurys, we had our penny but we knew not how to lay it out, there were gingerbread coaches & gingerbread milkmaids & to gratify two propensitys the taste & the fancy together we

129

bought one of these gilded toys & thought we had husbanded
our pennies well till they were gone & then we went away to
coax our parents for more thinking of better bargains when we
got money again.

   then there was Eastwell spring famous in those days for its
spaws & its brough at the fountain were we used to met of a
Sunday & have sugard drink   70
   & then came the sheep-shearing were we was sure of frumity   *a drink*
from the old shepherds if we sought the clipping-pens & lastly
came the harvest-home & its cross-skittles Ah what a paradise
begins with life & what a wilderness the knowledge of the
world discloses [. . .]

Composed 1824   First published 1951

   from SUMMER IMAGES

I love at early morn from new mown swath
To see the startled frog his rout pursue   100
And mark while leaping oer the dripping path
         His bright sides scatter dew
And early Lark that from its bustle flyes –
         To hail his mattin new
         And watch him to the skyes

And note on hedgerow baulks in moisture sprent
The jetty snail creep from the mossy thorn
In earnest heed and tremolous intent
         Frail brother of the morn
That from the tiney bents and misted leaves   110
         Withdraws his timid horn
         And fearful vision weaves

And swallows heed on smoke tanned chimney top
As wont be first unsealing morning's eye
Ere yet the bee hath gleaned one wayward drop
         Of honey on his thigh

And see him seek morn's airy couch to sing
    Untill the golden sky
    Besprents his russet wing

And sawning boy by tanning corn espy   120
With clapping noise to startle birds away
And hear him bawl to every passer bye
    To know the hour of day
And see the uncradled breeze refreshed and strong
    With waking blossoms play
    And breath eolian song

I love the south west wind or low or loud
And not the less when sudden drops of rain
Moistens my palid cheek from ebon cloud
    Threatning soft showers again   130
That over lands new ploughed and meadow grounds
    Summers sweet breath unchains
    And wakes harmonious sounds

Rich music breaths in summers every sound
And in her harmony of varied greens
Woods meadows hedgrows cornfields all around
    Much beauty intervenes
Filling with harmony the ear and eye
    While oer the mingling scenes
    Far spreads the laughing sky   140

And wind enarmourd Aspin – mark the leaves
Turn up their silver lining to the sun
And list the brustling noise that oft decieves
    And makes the sheep boy run
The sound so mimics fast approaching showers
    He thinks the rain begun
    And hastes to sheltering bowers

And mark the evening curdle dank and grey
Changing her watchet hue for sombre weeds   *light-blue*

131

And moping owls to close the lids of day 150
    On drowsy wing proceeds
While chickering cricket tremolous and long
    Lights farwell inly heeds
    And gives it parting song

While pranking bat its flighty circlet makes
And gloworm burnisheth its lamp anew
Oer meadow's dew besprent – and beetle wakes
    Enquiries ever new
Teazing each passing ear with murmurs vain
    As wonting to pursue 160
    His homward path again

And catch the melody of distant bells
That on the wind with pleasing hum rebounds
By fitful starts – then musically swells
    Oer the dim stilly grounds
While on the meadow bridge the pausing boy
    Listens the mellow sounds
    And hums in vacant joy

And now the homebound hedger bundles round
His evening faggot and with every stride 170
His leathern doublet leaves a rushing sound
    Till silly sheep beside
His path start tremolous – and once again
    Look back dissatisfied
    Then scour the dewy plain

Composed 1824–32   *First published 1835*

from THE SUMMER SHOWER

The plough team wet and dripping plashes home
And on the horse the ploughboy lolls along
Yet from the wet grounds come
The loud and merry song

Now neath the leafy arch of dripping bough
That loaded trees form oer the narrow lane
The horse released from plough
Naps the moist grass again   80

Around their blanket camps the gipseys still
Heedless of showers while black thorns shelter round
Jump oer the pasture hills
In many an idle bound

From dark green clumps among the dripping grain
The lark with sudden impulse starts and sings
And mid the smoking rain
Quivers her russet wings

A joy inspiring calmness all around
Breaths a refreshing sense of strengthening power   90
Like that which toil hath found
In sundays leisure hour

When spirits all relaxed heart sick of toil
Seeks out the pleasant woods and shadowy dells
And where the fountain boils
Lye listening distant bells

Amid the yellow furze the rabbits bed
Labour hath hid his tools and oer the heath
Hies to the milking shed
That stands the oak beneath   100

And there he wiles the pleasant shower away
Filling his mind with store of happy things
Rich crops of corn and hay
And all that plenty brings

The crampt horison now leans on the ground
Quiet and cool and labours hard employ
Ceases while all around
Falls a refreshing joy

Composed 1824–32   First published 1935

THE FLOOD

On Lolham Brigs in wild and lonely mood
Ive seen the winter floods their gambols play
Through each old arch that trembled while I stood
Bent oer its wall to watch the dashing spray
As their old stations would be washed away
Crash came the ice against the jambs and then
A shudder jarred the arches – yet once more
It breasted raving waves and stood agen
To wait the shock as stubborn as before
– While foam brown crested with the russet soil   10
As washed from new ploughed lands – would dart beneath
Then round and round a thousand eddies boil
On tother side – then pause as if for breath
One minute – and ingulphed – like life in death

Whose wrecky stains dart on the floods away
More swift then shadows in a stormy day
Things trail and turn and steady – all in vain
The engulphing arches shoot them quickly through
The feather dances flutters and again
Darts through the deepest dangers still afloat   20
Seeming as faireys whisked it from the view

134

And danced it oer the waves as pleasures boat
Light hearted as a merry thought in may –
Trays – uptorn bushes – fence demolished rails
Loaded with weeds in sluggish motions stray
Like water monsters lost each winds and trails
Till near the arches – then as in affright
It plunges – reels – and shudders out of sight

Waves trough – rebound – and fury boil again
Like plunging monsters rising underneath   30
Who at the top curl up a shaggy main
A moment catching at a surer breath
Then plunging headlong down and down – and on
Each following boil the shadow of the last
And other monsters rise when those are gone
Crest their fringed waves – plunge onward and are past
– The chill air comes around me ocean blea   *bleak*
From bank to bank the waterstrife is spread
Strange birds like snow spots oer the huzzing sea
Hang where the wild duck hurried past and fled   40
– On roars the flood – all restless to be free
Like trouble wandering to eternity — *An unusually abstract metaphor for Clare*

*Composed 1824–32   First published 1835 (verses 1, 3),
1935 (verse 2)*

MIST IN THE MEADOWS

The evening oer the meadow seems to stoop
More distant lessens the diminished spire
Mist in the hollows reaks and curdles up
Like fallen clouds that spread – and things retire
Less seen and less – the shepherd passes near
And little distant most grotesquely shades
As walking without legs – lost to his knees
As through the rawky creeping smoke he wades

foggy

135

Now half way up the arches dissappear
And small the bits of sky that glimmer through   10
Then trees loose all but tops – I meet the fields
And now the indistinctness passes bye
The shepherd all his length is seen again
And further on the village meets the eye

Composed 1824–32   First published 1935

EMMONSAILS HEATH IN WINTER

I love to see the old heath's withered brake
Mingle its crimpled leaves with furze and ling
While the old Heron from the lonely lake
Starts slow and flaps his melancholly wing
And oddling crow in idle motions swing
On the half-rotten ash trees topmost twig
Beside whose trunk the gipsey makes his bed —
Up flies the bouncing wood cock from the brig   *bridge*
Where a black quagmire quakes beneath the tread
The field fare chatters in the whistling thorn   10
And for the awe round fields and closen rove   *small fields*
And coy bumbarrels twenty in a drove   *small birds*
                                        (long-tailed tit)
Flit down the hedgerows in the frozen plain
And hang on little twigs and start again

haw-
thorn
berries

Composed 1824–32   First published 1908

ENGLAND, 1830

These vague allusions to a country's wrongs,
    Where one says 'Ay' and others answer 'No'
In contradiction from a thousand tongues,
    Till like to prison-cells her freedoms grow
Becobwebbed with these oft-repeated songs
    Of peace and plenty in the midst of woe –
And is it thus they mock her year by year,

136

Telling poor truth unto her face she lies,
Declaiming of her wealth with gibe severe,
   So long as taxes drain their wished supplies?   10
And will these jailers rivet every chain
   Anew, yet loudest in their mockery be,
To damn her into madness with disdain,
   Forging new bonds and bidding her be free?

Composed 1830   First published 1935

SCHOOLBOYS IN WINTER

The schoolboys still their morning rambles take
To neighbouring village school with playing speed,
Loitering with pastime's leisure till they quake,
Oft looking up the wild-geese droves to heed,
Watching the letters which their journeys make;
Or plucking haws on which the fieldfares feed,
And hips, and sloes; and on each shallow lake
Making glib slides, where they like shadows go   *smooth*
Till some fresh pastimes in their minds awake.
Then off they start anew and hasty blow   10
Their numbed and clumpsing fingers till they glow;
Then races with their shadows wildly run
That stride huge giants o'er the shining snow
In the pale splendour of the winter sun.

Composed 1824–32   First published 1924

THE FODDERING BOY

The foddering boy along the crumping snows
With straw-band-belted legs and folded arm
Hastens, and on the blast that keenly blows
Oft turns for breath, and beats his fingers warm,
And shakes the lodging snows from off his clothes,
Buttoning his doublet closer from the storm

137

*Of "Schoolboys in Winter," Lloyd Frankenberg
notes how it is Breughel-like in its observation.*

And slouching his brown beaver o'er his nose –
Then faces it agen, and seeks the stack
Within its circling fence where hungry lows
Expecting cattle, making many a track   10
About the snow, impatient for the sound
When in huge forkfuls trailing at his back
He litters the sweet hay about the ground
And brawls to call the staring cattle round.

Composed 1824–32   First published 1924

WINTER EVENING

The crib stock fothered – horses suppered up   *fed*
And cows in sheds all littered down in straw
The threshers gone the owls are left to whoop
The ducks go waddling with distended craw
Through little hole made in the henroost door
And geese with idle gabble never oer
Bate careless hog untill he tumbles down
Insult provoking spite to noise the more
While fowl high perched blink with contemptous frown
On all the noise and bother heard below   10
Over the stable ridge in crowds the crow
With jackdaws intermixed known by their noise
To the warm woods behind the village go
And whistling home for bed go weary boys

Composed 1824–32   First published 1935

SAND MARTIN

Thou hermit haunter of the lonely glen
And common wild and heath – the desolate face
Of rude waste landscapes far away from men
Where frequent quarrys give thee dwelling place
With strangest taste and labour undeterred

138

Drilling small holes along the quarrys side
More like the haunts of vermin than a bird
And seldom by the nesting boy descried
Ive seen thee far away from all thy tribe
Flirting about the unfrequented sky   10
And felt a feeling that I cant describe
Of lone seclusion and a hermit joy
To see thee circle round nor go beyond
That lone heath and its melancholly pond

Composed 1824–32   First published 1935

THE THRUSHES NEST

Within a thick and spreading awthorn bush   *hawthorn*
That overhung a molehill large and round
I heard from morn to morn a merry thrush
Sing hymns to sunrise while I drank the sound
With joy and often an intruding guest
I watched her secret toils from day to day
How true she warped the moss to form her nest
And modelled it within with wood and clay
And bye and bye like heath bells gilt with dew
There lay her shining eggs as bright as flowers   10
Ink-spotted over shells of greeny blue
And there I witnessed in the summer hours
A brood of natures minstrels chirp and fly
Glad as the sunshine and the laughing sky

Composed 1824–32   First published 1835

THE PETTICHAPS NEST   *Also called willow-warbler*

Well in my many walks I rarely found
A place less likely for a bird to form
Its nest close by the rut gulled waggon road
And on the almost bare foot-trodden ground

With scarce a clump of grass to keep it warm
And not a thistle spreads its spears abroad
Or prickly bush to shield it from harms way
And yet so snugly made that none may spy
It out save accident – and you and I
Had surely passed it in our walk to day   10
Had chance not led us by it – nay e'en now
Had not the old bird heard us trampling bye
And fluttered out – we had not seen it lie
Brown as the road way side – small bits of hay
Pluckt from the old propt-haystacks pleachy brow
And withered leaves make up its outward walls
That from the snub-oak dotterel yearly falls
And in the old hedge bottom rot away
Built like a oven with a little hole
Hard to discover – that snug entrance wins   20
Scarcely admitting e'en two fingers in
And lined with feathers warm as silken stole
And soft as seats of down for painless ease
And full of eggs scarce bigger e'en then peas   *than*
Heres one most delicate with spots as small
As dust – and of a faint and pinky red
– We'll let them be and safety guard them well
For fears rude paths around are thickly spread
And they are left to many dangers ways
When green grass hoppers jump might break the shells   30
While lowing oxen pass them morn and night
And restless sheep around them hourly stray
And no grass springs but hungry horses bite
That trample past them twenty times a day
Yet like a miracle in safetys lap
They still abide unhurt and out of sight
– Stop,heres the bird that woodman at the gap
Hath frit it from the hedge – tis olive green   *frightened*
Well I declare it is the pettichaps
Not bigger then the wren and seldom seen   40

I've often found their nests in chance's way
When I in pathless woods did idly roam
But never did I dream untill to day
A spot like this would be her chosen home

Composed 1824–32   First published 1835

THE YELLOWHAMMER'S NEST

= Flicker

Frightened

Just by the wooden brig a bird flew up
Frit by the cowboy as he scrambled down
To reach the misty dewberry — let us stoop
And seek its nest — the brook we need not dread
Tis scarcely deep enough a bee to drown
So it sings harmless oer its pebbly bed
— Aye here it is stuck close beside the bank
Beneath the bunch of grass that spindles rank
Its husk seeds tall and high — tis rudely planned
Of bleached stubbles and the withered fare   10
That last year's harvest left upon the land
Lined thinly with the horse's sable hair
— Five eggs pen-scribbled over lilac shells
Resembling writing scrawls which fancy reads
As natures poesy and pastoral spells
They are the yellow hammers and she dwells
A poet-like — where brooks and flowery weeds
As sweet as Castaly to fancy seems
And that old molehill like as parnass hill   Mount Parnassus
On which her partner haply sits and dreams   20
Oer all his joy of song — so leave it still
A happy home of sunshine flowers and streams
Yet in the sweetest places cometh ill
A noisome weed that burthens every soil
For snakes are known with chill and deadly coil
To watch such nests and seize the helpless young

And like as though the plague became a guest
Leaving a housless-home a ruined nest
And mournful hath the little warblers sung
When such like woes hath rent its little breast   30

Composed 1824–32   First published 1835

'SNAKES'

I do not know how to class the venemous animals further then   than
by the vulgar notion of putting toads, common snakes, black
snakes (calld by the Peasantry Vipers), Newts (often calld
eatherns), and a nimble scaly looking newt-like thing about the
lizards heaths calld Swifts by the furze kidders and cow keepers. all   bundlers of furze
these we posses in troublsome quantitys, all of which is reckond
poisonous by the common people, tho a many daring people has
provd that the common snake is not, for I have seen men with
whom I have workd in the fields take them up and snatch them
out of joint (as they calld it) in a moment, so that when they was   10
thrown down they coud not stir but lay and dyd. others will
take them up in one hand and hold the other agen that double
tongue pointed fang which they put out in a threatning manner when
pursued and which is erroniously calld their sting, and when it
touches the hand it appears utterly harmless and turns again as
weak as an horse hair. yet still they are calld poisonous and
dreaded by many people and I myself cannot divest my feelings
of their first impressions tho I have been convincd to the contrary. we have them about us in great quantitys. they even
come in the village and breed in the dung-hills in farm yards   20
and harbour in old walls. they are fond of lying rolld up like a
whipthong in the sun. they seem to be always jealous of   wary
danger as they never lye far from their hiding places and retreat
in a moment at the least noise or sound of approaching
feet. they lay a great number of eggs white and large. the
shell is a skinny substance and full of glutiness matter like the
white in birds eggs, they hang together by hundreds as if

142

strung on a string. they lay them on the south side of old dung-
hills <u>were</u> the heat of the sun and the dung together hatches
them. when they first leave the shells they are no thicker then a
worsted needle or bodkin. they nimble about after the old
snakes and if they are in danger the old ones open their mouths
and the young dissapear down their throats in a moment till the
danger is over and then they come out and run about as usual. I
have not seen this myself but I am as certain of it as if I had
because I have heard it told so often by those that did. when I
have been <u>pilling</u> bark in the woods in oaking time I have seen
snakes creeping half errect by the sides of the fallen oaks that
were pilld putting their darting horse-hair-like tongue every
now and then to the tree,and I was a long while ere I coud make
out what they were doing,but I made it out at last in my mind
that they were catching flyes that were attracted there in great
quantitys to the moister of the sap just after the bark had been
ripd off – this I have observd many times and I think if it were
examind they have a sticky moister at the end of those double
ended fangs that appears like a bit of wailbone split at the end or
a double horse hair which attaches to the flye as soon as touchd
like bird lime and I think this is the use for which nature designd
their mistaken stings. the motion was so quick that the prey
which it seizd coud not be percievd when taken but I have not
the least doubt that such was its object. people talk about the
Watersnake but I cannot believe otherwise then that the water
and land snake are one,tho I have killd snakes by the water in
meadows of a different and more deep color then those I have
found in the fields. the water snake will swallow very large
frogs. I have often known them to be ripd out of their bellys by
those who have skind the snake to wear the skin round their
hats which is reckond as a charm against the headach and is
often tryd but with what success I am not able to say. some say
that snakes are as wholsom as eels to eat and when the french
prisoners were at Norman cross Barracks it was a very common
thing among the people of the villages round to go in the fens a
snake-catching and carry home large sticks of them strung like
eels on osiers which the French men woud readily buy as an

where

30

peeling

40

50

60

143

article of very palatable food, I know this to be a fact but I
rather doubt the frenchmen's good taste in cookery by eating
such things – the fens swarm with snakes, I have walkd by the
brink of a large dyke among the long grass in a morning when
they have ran away from every step I took and dropt into the
water by scores   the Fenmen care nothing about them no more   70
then childern do for the common flye, when we see any we kill
them and think we get rid of a danger by so doing but the fen
people pass them without fear or notice, in fact if they dreaded
them they coud not stir out of their doors they are so numerous
there, The black snake or Viper a very small one about a foot
long and not often thicker <u>then</u> ones little finger is very scarce   *than*
here and venemous, I believe the fens have none; they seem to
inhabit high land, a place calld Southey wood is a spot were
they are oftenest seen with us, a woodman got stung by one in
worthorp Groves near Burghley some few years ago and his   80
hand and arm swelld very large, another man while cutting up
furze on a place calld the Lings at Casterton was stung over the
leg by one and lay ill a long time, and when I was a boy I can
remember a next-door neighbour named Landon was stung
with one of these vipers in crossing a close of long grass, he
describd the sensation as if a thorn had prickd him just above his
shoe top on the ancle and shoud have believd it had been so had
not his wife been following him who saw at the moment
somthing hustle quickly in the grass when she told him and he
turnd back and killd it with his stick, on coming up to some   90
gipseys they advisd him to take the dead viper home to boil it
and apply the broth to the wound which he did but it got worse
and worse and the doctors when they saw it expected it woud
have mortified but he got well – I have seen three of these black
snakes, they are very quick-eyd looking things with a fang
darting out like the common ones, their heads are shorter and
much flatter then the large snake and their colors are more deep
and bright, their backs are black and their bellys bright yellow
interspersd with scaly bars of blackish hues – I have heard some
people affirm that even these are not venom[ous] and that   100
people who suppose themselves bitten by them mistake sudden

yumours falling in their limbs for a bite. I believe this is the
Docters'opinion with us – all I can say is that I never was harmd
by them [. . .]

Composed 1824   First published 1951

HEDGE SPARROW

The tame hedge sparrow in its russet dress
Is half a robin for its gentle ways
And the bird loving dame can do no less
Then throw it out a crumble on cold days
In early march it into gardens strays
And in the snug clipt box tree green and round
It makes a nest of moss and hair and lays
When een the snow is lurking on the ground
Its eggs in number five of greenish blue
Bright beautiful and glossy shining shells   10
Much like the firetails but of brighter hue
Yet in her garden home much danger dwells
Where skulking cat with mischief in its breast
Catches their young before they leave the nest

Composed 1824–32   First published 1935

from THE FLITTING

Give me no high flown fangled things
No haughty pomp in marching chime
Where muses play on golden strings
And splendour passes for sublime
Where citys stretch as far as fame
And fancys straining eye can go
And piled untill the sky for shame
Is stooping far away below   160

I love the verse that mild and bland
Breaths of green fields and open sky
I love the muse that in her hand
Bears wreaths of native poesy
Who walks nor skips the pasture brook
In scorn – but by the drinking horse
Leans oer its little brig to look   *bridge*
How far the sallows lean accross   *willows*

And feels a rapture in her breast
Upon their root-fringed grains to mark   170
A hermit morehens sedgy nest
Just like a naiads summer bark
She counts the eggs she cannot reach
Admires the spot and loves it well
And yearns so natures lessons teach
Amid such neighbourhoods to dwell

I love the muse who sits her down
Upon the molehills little lap
Who feels no fear to stain her gown
And pauses by the hedgerow gap   180
Not with that affectation praise
Of song to sing and never see
A field flower grow in all her days
Or e'en a forests aged tree

E'en here my simple feelings nurse
A love for every simple weed
And e'en this little shepherds purse
Grieves me to cut it up – Indeed
I feel at times a love and joy
For every weed and every thing   190
A feeling kindred from a boy
A feeling brought with every spring

And why – this 'shepherds purse' that grows
In this strange spot in days gone bye

Grew in the little garden rows
Of that old hut now left – and I
Feel what I never felt before
This weed an ancient neighbour here
And though I own the spot no more
Its every trifle makes it dear   200

The ivy at the parlour end
The woodbine at the garden gate
Are all and each affection's friend
That renders parting desolate
But times will change and friends must part
And nature still can make amends
Their memory lingers round the heart
Like life whose essence is its friends

Time looks on pomp with careless moods
Or killing apathy's disdain   210
– So where old marble cities stood
Poor persecuted weeds remain
She feels a love for little things
That very few can feel beside
And still the grass eternal springs
Where castles stood and grandeur died

Composed 1832   First published 1908

REMEMBRANCES

Summer pleasures they are gone like to visions every one
And the cloudy days of autumn and of winter cometh on
I tried to call them back but unbidden they are gone
Far away from heart and eye and for ever far away
Dear heart and can it be that such raptures meet decay
I thought them all eternal when by Langley bush I lay
I thought them joys eternal when I used to shout and play

On its bank at 'clink and bandy' 'chock' and 'taw' and children's game
   ducking stone
Where silence sitteth now on the wild heath as her own
Like a ruin of the past all alone   10

When I used to lie and sing by old eastwells boiling spring
When I used to tie the willow boughs together for a 'swing'
And fish with crooked pins and thread and never catch a
   thing
With heart just like a feather – now as heavy as a stone
When beneath old lea close oak I the bottom branches broke
To make our harvest cart like so many working folk
And then to cut a straw at the brook to have a soak
O I never dreamed of parting or that trouble had a sting
Or that pleasures like a flock of birds would ever take to
   wing
Leaving nothing but a little naked spring   20

When jumping time away on old cross berry way
And eating <u>awes</u> like sugar plumbs ere they had lost the may haws
And skipping like a leveret before the peep of day
On the rolly polly up and downs of pleasant swordy well
When in round oaks narrow lane as the south got black again
We sought the hollow ash that was shelter from the rain
With our pockets full of peas we had stolen from the grain
How delicious was the dinner time on such a showry day
O words are poor receipts for what time hath stole away
The ancient pulpit trees and the play   30

When for school o'er 'little field' with its brook and wooden
   <u>brig</u>   bridge
Where I swaggered like a man though I was not half so big
While I held my little plough though twas but a willow twig
And drove my team along made of nothing but a name
'Gee hep' and 'hoit' and 'woi' – O I never call to mind
These pleasant names of places but I leave a sigh behind
While I see the litle <u>mouldywharps</u> hang <u>sweeing</u> to the wind

148   moles   swinging

On the only aged willow that in all the field remains
And nature hides her face where theyre sweeing in their
    chains
And in a silent murmuring complains   40

Here was commons for their hills where they seek for
    freedom still
Though every commons gone and though traps are set to kill
The little homeless miners – O it turns my bosom chill
When I think of old 'sneap green' puddocks nook and hilly
    snow
Where bramble bushes grew and the daisy gemmed in dew
And the hills of silken grass like to cushions to the view
Where we threw the pissmire crumbs when we'd nothing   *ant*
    else to do
All leveled like a desert by the never weary plough
All vanished like the sun where that cloud is passing now
All settled here for ever on its brow   50

O I never thought that joys would run away from boys
Or that boys would change their minds and forsake such
    summer joys
But alack I never dreamed that the world had other toys
To petrify first feelings like the fable into stone
Till I found the pleasure past and a winter come at last
Then the fields were sudden bare and the sky got overcast
And boyhoods pleasing haunts like a blossom in the blast
Was shrivelled to a withered weed and trampled down and
    done
Till vanished was the morning spring and set that summer
    sun
And winter fought her battle strife and won   60

By Langley bush I roam but the bush hath left its hill
On cowper green I stray tis a desert strange and chill
And spreading lea close oak ere decay had penned its will
To the axe of the spoiler and self interest fell a prey

And cross berry way and old round oaks narrow lane
With its hollow trees like pulpits I shall never see again
Inclosure like a Buonaparte let not a thing remain
It levelled every bush and tree and levelled every hill
And hung the moles for traitors – though the brook is
    running still
It runs a naked brook cold and chill   70

O had I known as then joy had left the paths of men
I had watched her night and day besure and never slept agen
And when she turned to go O I'd caught her mantle then
And wooed her like a lover by my lonely side to stay
Aye knelt and worshiped on as love in beauty's bower
And clung upon her smiles as a bee upon a flower
And gave her heart my poesys all cropt in a sunny hour
As keepsakes and pledges all to never fade away
But love never heeded to treasure up the may
So it went the common road with decay   80

Composed c. 1832   First published 1908

THE FENS

Wandering by the river's edge
I love to rustle through the sedge
And through the woods of reed to tear
Almost as high as bushes are
Yet turning quick with shudder chill
As danger ever does from ill
Fears moment ague quakes the blood
While plop the snake coils in the flood
And hissing with a forked tongue
Across the river winds along   10

In coat of orange green and blue
Now on a willow branch I view
Grey waving to the sunny gleam

King fishers watch the ripple stream
For little fish that nimble bye
And in the gravel shallows lie

Eddies run before the boats
Gurgling where the fisher floats
Who takes advantage of the gale
And hoists his hankerchief for sail   20
On osier twigs that form a mast
And quick his nutshell hurrys past
While idly lies nor wanted more
The spirit that pushed him on before

There not a hill in all the view
Save that a forked cloud or two
Upon the verge of distance lies
And into mountains cheats the eyes
And as to trees the willows wear
Lopped heads as high as bushes are   30
Some taller things the distance shrouds
That may be trees or stacks or clouds
Or may be nothing still they wear
A zemblance where theres nought to spare

Among the tawny tasseled reed
The ducks and ducklings float and feed
With head oft dabbing in the flood
They fish all day the weedy mud
And tumbler like are bobbing there
Tails topsy turvy in the air   40
Then up and quack and down they go
Heels over head again below
The geese in troops come droving up
Nibble the weeds and take a sup
And closely puzzled to agree
Chatter like gossips over tea
The ganders with their scarlet nose

When strife gets highest interpose
And strecking necks to that and this
With now a mutter now a hiss   50
A nibble at the feathers too
A sort of pray be quiet do
And turning as the matter mends
He stills them into mutual friends
Then in a sort of triumph sings
And throws the water oer his wings
Ah could I see a spinny nigh
A puddock sailing in the sky   k.Te
Above the oaks with easy sail
On stilly wing and forked tail   60
Or meet a heath of furze in flower
I might enjoy a pleasant hour
Sit down at rest and walk at ease
And find a many things to please
But here my fancys moods admire
The naked levels till they tire
Nor een a molehill cushion meets
To rest on when I want a seat

Heres little save the river scene
And grounds of oats in smiling green   70
And crowded growth of wheat and beans
That with the hope of plenty leans
And cheers the farmers gazing brow
Who lives and triumphs in the plough
One sometimes meets a pleasant sward
Of swarthy grass – and quickly marred
The plough soon turns it into brown
And when again one rambles down
The path small hillocks lie
And smoak beneath a burning sky   80
Green paddocks have but little charms
With gain the merchandise of farms
And muse and marvel where we may

152

Gain mars the landscape every day
The meadow grass turned up and copt
The trees to stumpy <u>dotterels</u> lopt   *pollardized trees*
The hearth with fuel to supply
For rest to smoke and chatter bye
Giving the joy of home delights
The warmest mirth on coldest nights   90
And so for gain that joys repay
Change cheats the landscape every day
No tree no bough about it grows
That from the hatchet can repose
And the orison stooping smiles
Oer treeless fens of many miles
Spring comes and goes and comes again
And all is nakedness and fen

And dunghills hiding snake and toad
Lyes more then half accross the road   100
Where docks and thistles crowd the lane
Cut yearly yet they come again
And those the quaking winter finds
Make dithering whistles on the wind
Picturing to passengers acold
A picture dreary to behold
Where spite of all they eat and kill
A scene that makes the cold achill
Large grounds bethronged with thistles brown
Shivering and swadding up and down   110
Was but a bramble in the place
Twould be a sort of living grace
A shape of shelter in the wind
For stock to chew their cuds behind
But all is level cold and dull
And osier swamps with water full

Composed 1832–7   First published 1920

153

THE RAGWORT

Ragwort thou humble flower with tattered leaves
I love to see thee come and litter gold
What time the summer binds her russet sheaves
Decking rude spots in beauty's marigold
That without thee were dreary to behold
Sun burnt and bare – the meadow bank the <u>baulk</u>   *strip of grass dividing fields*
That leads a waggonway through mellow fields
Rich with the tints that harvest's plenty yields
Browns of all hues – and every where I walk
Thy waste of shining blossoms richly shields   10
The sun-tanned sward in splendid hues that burn
So bright and glaring that the very light
Of the rich sunshine doth to paleness turn
And seems but very shadows in thy sight

Composed 1832–7   First published 1924

Unusual rhyme scheme for a sonnet:
ababb
cddcd
e fef

THE MOUSE'S NEST

I found a ball of grass among the hay
And <u>proged</u> it as I passed and went away   *prodded*
And when I looked I fancied somthing stirred
And turned agen and hoped to catch the bird
When out an old mouse bolted in the wheat
With all her young ones hanging at her teats
She looked so odd and so grotesque to me
I ran and wondered what the thing could be
And pushed the knapweed bunches where I stood
When the mouse hurried from the crawling brood   10
The young ones squeaked and when I went away
She found her nest again among the hay
The water oer the pebbles scarce could run } *Strange ending,*
And broad old cesspools glittered in the sun } *even for a sonnet*

Composed 1832–7   First published 1935

154

SHEEP IN WINTER

The sheep get up and make their many tracks
And bear a load of snow upon their backs
And gnaw the frozen turnip to the ground
With sharp quick bite and then go noising round
The boy that pecks the turnips all the day
And knocks his hands to keep the cold away
And laps his legs in straw to keep them warm
And hides behind the hedges from the storm
The sheep as tame as dogs go where he goes
And try to shake their fleeces from the snows   10
Then leave their frozen meal and wander round
The stubble stack that stands beside the ground
And lye all night and face the drizzling storm
And shun the hovel where they might be warm

Composed 1832–7   First published 1935

WILD BEES' NEST

The mower tramples on the wild bees' nest
And hears the busy noise and stops the rest
Who carless proggle out the mossy ball   *prods*
And gather up the honey comb and all
The boy that seeks dewberrys from the sedge
And lays the poison berrys on the hedge
Will often find them in the meadow hay
And take his bough and drive the bees away
But when the maiden goes to turn the hay
She whips her apron up and runs away   10
The schoolboy eats the honey comb and all
And often knocks his hat agen the wall
And progs a stick in every hole he sees   *prods*
To steal the honey bag of black nosed bees

Composed 1832–7   First published 1935

155

STONE PIT

The passing traveller with wonder sees
A deep and ancient stone pit full of trees
So deep and very deep the place has been
The church might stand within and not be seen
The passing stranger oft with wonder stops
And thinks he een could walk upon <u>their</u> tops   *i.e., the trees'*
And often stoops to see the busy crow
And stands above and sees the eggs below
And while the wild horse gives his head a toss
The squirrel dances up and runs accross   10
The boy that stands and kills the black nosed bee
Dares down as soon as magpies nests are found
And wonders when he climbs the highest tree
To find it reaches scarce above the ground

Composed 1832–7   First published 1920

WILD DUCK'S NEST

As boys where playing in their schools dislike
And floating paper boats along the dyke
They laid their baskets down a nest to see
And found a small hole in a hollow tree
When one looked in and wonder filled his breast
And halloed out a wild duck on her nest
They doubted and the boldest went before
And the duck bolted when they waded oer
And <u>suthied</u> up and flew against the wind   *made a rushing nois*
And left the boys and wondering thoughts behind   10
The eggs lay hid in down and lightly prest
They counted more then thirty in the nest
They filled their hats with eggs and waded oer
And left the nest as quiet as before

Composed 1832–7   First published 1935

156

The green woodpecker flying up and down
With wings of mellow green and speckled crown
She bores a hole in trees with crawking noise
And pelted down and often catched by boys
She makes a <u>lither</u> nest of grass and whool   *lazy*
Men fright her oft that go the sticks to pull
Ive up and clumb the trees with hook and pole
And stood on rotten grains to reach the hole
And as I trembled upon fear and doubt
I found the eggs and scarce could get them out   10
I put them in my hat a tattered crown
And scarcely without breaking brought them down
The eggs are small for such a bird they lay
Five eggs and like the sparrows spotted grey

Composed 1832–7   First published 1973

WOODPECKER'S NEST

There is a small woodpecker red and grey
That hides in woods and forrests far away
They run like creepers up and down the tree
And few can find them when they stand to see
They seldom fly away but run and climb
A man may stand and look for twenty time
And seldom see them once for half a day
Ive stood nor seen them till they flew away
Ive swarmed the grain and clumb with hook and pole
But scarce could get three fingers in the hole   10
They build on grains scarse thicker then ones legs
Ive found the nests but never got the eggs
But boys who wish to see what eggs they lay
Will climb the tree and saw the grain away

Composed 1832–7   First published 1973

THE PUDDOCK'S NEST

The sailing puddock sweeps about for prey
And keeps above the woods from day to day
They make a nest so large in woods remote
Would fill a woman's apron with the sprotes
And schoolboys daring doing tasks the best
Will often climb and stand upon the nest
They find a hugh old tree and free from snaggs
And make a flat nest lined with wool and rags
And almost big enough to make a bed
And lay three eggs and spotted oer with red   10
The schoolboy often hears the old ones cry
And climbs the tree and gets them ere they fly
And takes them home and often cuts their wing
And ties them in the garden with a string

Composed 1832–7   *First published 1973*

THE GROUNDLARK

Close where the milking maidens pass
In roots and <u>twitches</u> drest   *couch grass*
Within a little bunch of grass
A groundlark made her nest
The maiden touched her with her gown
And often <u>frit</u> her out   *frightened*
And looked and set her buckets down
But never found it out
The eggs where large and spotted round
And dark as is the fallow ground   10
The schoolboy kicked the grass in play
But danger never guest
And when they came to mow the hay
They found an empty nest

Composed 1832–7   *First published 1935*

THE MARTEN

The martin cat long shaged of courage good
Of weazle shape a dweller in the wood
With badger hair long shagged and darting eyes
And lower then the common cat in size
Small head and running on the stoop
Snuffing the ground and hind parts shouldered up
He keeps one track and hides in lonely shade
Where print of human foot is scarcely made
Save when the woods are cut the beaten track
The woodmans dog will snuff cock tailed and black   10
Red legged and spotted over either eye
Snuffs barks and scrats the tree and passes bye
The great brown horned owl looks down below
And sees the shaggy martin come and go

The martin hurrys through the woodland gaps
And poachers shoot and make his skin for caps
When any woodman come and pass the place
He looks at dogs and scarcely mends his pace
And gipseys often and birdnesting boys
Look in the hole and hear a hissing noise   20
They climb the tree such noise they never heard
And think the great owl is a foreign bird
When the grey owl her young ones cloathed in down
Seizes the boldest boy and drives him down
They try agen and pelt to start the fray
The grey owl comes and drives them all away
And leaves the martin twisting round his den
Left free from boys and dogs and noise and men

Composed 1835–7   First published 1924

Handwritten annotations:
Repetition evidence of incompletion

scratches

159

THE FOX

The shepherd on his journey heard when nigh
His dog among the bushes barking high
The ploughman ran and gave a hearty shout
He found a weary fox and beat him out
The ploughman laughed and would have ploughed him in
But the old shepherd took him for the skin
He lay upon the furrow stretched and dead
The old dog lay and licked the wounds that bled
The ploughman beat him till his ribs would crack
And then the shepherd slung him at his back   10
And when he rested to his dog's supprise
The old fox started from his dead disguise
And while the dog lay panting in the sedge
He up and snapt and bolted through the hedge

He scampered [to] the bushes far away
The shepherd call[ed] the ploughman [to] the fray
The ploughman wished he had a gun to shoot
The old dog barked and followed the pursuit
The shepherd threw his hook and tottered past
The ploughman ran but none could go so fast   20
The woodman threw his faggot from the way
And ceased to chop and wondered at the fray
But when he saw the dog and heard the cry
He threw his hatchet but the fox was bye
The shepherd broke his hook and lost the skin
He found a badger hole and bolted in
They tryed to dig but safe from danger's way
He lived to chase the hounds another day

Composed 1835–7   First published 1920

THE BADGER

The badger grunting on his woodland track
With shaggy hide and sharp nose scrowed with black   *marked*
Roots in the bushes and the woods and makes
A great hugh burrow in the ferns and brakes   *bracken*
With nose on ground he runs a awkard pace
And anything will beat him in the race
The shepherds dog will run him to his den
Followed and hooted by the dogs and men
The woodman when the hunting comes about
Go round at night to stop the foxes out   10
And hurrying through the bushes ferns and brakes
Nor sees the many holes the badger makes
And often through the bushes to the chin
Breaks the old holes and tumbles headlong in

When midnight comes a host of dogs and men
Go out and track the badger to his den
And put a sack within the hole and lye
Till the old grunting badger passes bye
He comes and hears they let the strongest loose
The old fox hears the noise and drops the goose   20
The poacher shoots and hurrys from the cry
And the old hare half wounded buzzes bye
They get a forked stick to bear him down
And clapt the dogs and bore him to the town
And bait him all the day with many dogs
And laugh and shout and fright the scampering hogs
He runs along and bites at all he meets
They shout and hollo down the noisey streets

He turns about to face the loud uproar
And drives the rebels to their very doors   30
The frequent stone is hurled where ere they go
When badgers fight and every ones a foe
The dogs are clapt and urged to join the fray
The badger turns and drives them all away

Though scarcely half as big <u>dimute</u> and small   *diminutive*
He fights with dogs for hours and beats them all
The heavy mastiff savage in the fray
Lies down and licks his feet and turns away
The bull dog knows his match and waxes cold
The badger grins and never leaves his hold   40
He drives the crowd and follows at their heels
And bites them through the drunkard swears and reels

The frighted women takes the boys away
The blackguard laughs and hurrys on the fray
He trys to reach the woods a awkard race
But sticks and cudgels quickly stop the chace
He turns agen and drives the noisey crowd
And beats the many dogs in noises loud
He drives away and beats them every one
And then they loose them all and set them on   50
He falls as dead and kicked by boys and men
Then starts and grins and drives the crowd agen
Till kicked and torn and beaten out he lies
And leaves his hold and cackles groans and dies

Some keep a baited badger tame as hog
And tame him till he follows like the dog
They urge him on like dogs and show fair play
He beats and scarcely wounded goes away
Lapt up as if asleep he scorns to fly
And siezes any dog that ventures nigh
Clapt like a dog he never bites the men
But worrys dogs and hurrys to his den
They let him out and turn a barrow down
And there he fights the pack of all the town
He licks the patting hand and trys to play
And never trys to bite or run away
And runs away from noise in hollow trees
Burnt by the boys to get a swarm of bees

Anticlimactic, but interesting in its own way as an example of how man 60 *can tame a creature that would be better left in wildness*

Composed 1835–7   First published 1920

162

THE HEDGEHOG

The hedgehog hides beneath the rotten hedge
And makes a great round nest of grass and sedge
Or in a bush or in a hollow tree
And many often stoops and say they see
Him roll and fill his prickles full of crabs   *spines, crabapples*
And creep away and where the magpie dabs
His wing at muddy dyke in aged root
He makes a nest and fills it full of fruit
On the hedge bottom hunts for crabs and sloes   *sloeberries*
And whistles like a cricket as he goes   10
It rolls up like a ball a shapeless hog
When gipseys hunt it with their noisey dogs
Ive seen it in their camps they call it sweet
Though black and bitter and unsavoury meat

But they who hunt the fields for rotten meat   *i.e, gypsies*
And wash in muddy dyke and call it sweet
And eat what dogs refuse where ere they dwell
Care little either for the taste or smell
They say they milk the cows and when they lye
Nibble their fleshy teats and make them dry   20
But they whove seen the small head like a hog
Rolled up to meet the savage of a dog
With mouth scarce big enough to hold a straw
Will neer believe what no one ever saw
But still they hunt the hedges all about
And shepherd dogs are trained to hunt them out
They hurl with savage force the stick and stone
And no one cares and still the strife goes on

Composed 1835–7   First published 1935

THE VIXEN

Among the taller wood with ivy hung
The old fox plays and dances round her young
She snuffs and barks if any passes bye
And swings her tail and turns prepared to flye
The horseman hurrys bye she bolts to see
And turns agen from danger never free
If any stands she runs among the poles   *i,e,, any of her cubs*
And barks and snaps and drives them in the holes
The shepherd sees them and the boy goes bye
And gets a stick and progs the hole to try   *prods*   10
They get all still and lie in safty sure
And out again when safety is secure
And start and snap at blackbirds bouncing bye
To fight and catch the great white butterflye

Composed 1835–7   First published 1920

THE WATER LILIES

The Water Lilies, white and yellow flowers,
    How beautiful they are upon the lake!
I've stood and looked upon the place for hours,
    And thought how fine a garden they would make.
The pleasant leaves upon the water float;
    The dragon-fly would come and stay for hours,
And when the water pushed the pleasure boat,
    Would find a safer place among the flowers:
They lay like Pleasure in a quiet place,
    Close where the moor-hen loved her nest to make, –   10
They lay like beauty with a smiling face,
    And I have called them 'Ladies of the Lake!'
I've brought the longest pole and stood for hours,
And tried for years, before I got those flowers!

Composed 1840–1   First published 1841

164

THE GIPSY CAMP

The snow falls deep; the Forest lies alone:
The boy goes hasty for his load of brakes,
Then thinks upon the fire and hurries back;
The Gipsy knocks his hands and tucks them up,
And seeks his squalid camp, half hid in snow,
Beneath the oak, which breaks away the wind,
And bushes close, with snow like hovel warm:
There stinking mutton roasts upon the coals,
And the half-roasted dog squats close and rubs,
Then feels the heat too strong and goes aloof;   10
He watches well, but none a bit can spare,
And vainly waits the morsel thrown away:
'Tis thus they live – a picture to the place;
A quiet, pilfering, unprotected race.

Composed 1840–1   First published 1841

LONDON VERSUS EPPING FOREST

The brakes, like young stag's horns, come up in Spring,   *bracken*
And hide the rabbit holes and fox's den;
They crowd about the forest everywhere;
The ling and holly-bush, and woods of beach,   *beech*
With room enough to walk and search for flowers;
Then look away and see the Kentish heights.
Nature is lofty in her better mood,
She leaves the world and greatness all behind;
Thus London, like a shrub among the hills,
Lies hid and lower than the bushes here.   10
I could not bear to see the tearing plough
Root up and steal the Forest from the poor,
But leave to freedom all she loves, untamed,
The Forest walk enjoyed and loved by all!

Composed 1840–1   First published 1841

'BYRON'S FUNERAL'

[. . .] while I was in London the melancholly death of Lord
Byron was announced in the public papers & I saw his remains
born away out of the city on its last journey to that place were   *where*
fame never comes tho it lives like a shadow & lingers like a sun-
beam on his grave it cannot enter therefore it is a victory that
has won nothing to the victor his funeral was blazed forth in
the papers with the usual parade that accompanys the death of
great men I happend to see it by chance as I was wandering up
Oxford street on my way to Mrs Emmersons when my eye was
suddenly arested by straggling gropes of the common people   10 *gro*
collected together & talking about a funeral I did as the rest did
tho I coud not get hold of what funeral it coud be but I knew it
was not a common one by the curiosity that kept watch on
every countenance bye & bye the grope collected into about a
hundred or more when the train of a funeral suddenly appeard
on which a young girl that stood beside me gave a deep sigh &
utterd Poor Lord Byron there was a mellancholy feeling of
vanity for great names never are at a loss for flatterers that as
every flower has its insect they dance in the sunbeams to share a
liliputian portion of its splendour upon most countenances I   20
looked up in the young girls face it was dark & beautiful & I
could almost feel in love with her for the sigh she had utterd
for the poet it was worth all the Newspaper puffs & Magazine
Mournings that ever was paraded after the death of a poet since
flattery & hypocrisy was babtizd in the name of truth & sin-
cerity – the Reverend the Moral & fastidious may say what
they please about Lord Byrons fame & damn it as they [please]
– he has gaind the path of its eternity without them & lives
above the blight of their mildewing censure to do him damage
– the common people felt his merits & his power & the   30
common people of a country are the best feelings of a prophecy
of futurity they are the veins & arterys that feed & quicken the
heart of living fame the breathings of eternity & the soul of
time are indicated in that prophecy they did not stand gaping
with suprise on the trappings & gaudy show (for there was not

166

much appearance of that it looked like a neglected grandeur) or
look on with apathisd indifference like the hird mutes in the
spectacle but they felt it I coud see it in their faces they stood in
profound silence till it passd not enquiring what this was or
that was about the show as they do at the shadow of welth &   40
gaudy trappings of a common great name – they felt by a natural
impulse that the mighty was fallen & they movd in saddend
silence the streets were lined as the procession passed on each
side but they were all the commonest & the lower orders I was
supprisd & gratified the windows & doors had those of the
higher [orders] about them but they wore smiles on their faces
& thought more of the spectacle then of the poet – the young   *than*
girl that stood by me had counted the carriages in her mind as
they passd & she told me there was 63 or 4 in all they were of all
sorts & sizes & made up a motly show the gilt ones that led the   50
processions were empty – the hearse lookd small & rather mean
& the coach that followd carried his em[bers] in a urn over   *ashes*
which a pawl was thrown tho one might distinguish the form
of the [urn] underneath & the window seemd to be left open for
that purpose – I believe that his liberal principals in religion &
politics did a great deal towards gaining the notice & affections
of the lower orders be as it will it is better to be beloved by those
low & humble for undisguised honesty then flattered by the
great for purchased & pensiond hypocrisy – [. . .]

Composed 1825   First published 1951

DON JUAN A POEM

'Poets are born' – and so are whores – the trade is
Grown universal – in these canting days
Women of fashion must of course be ladies
And whoreing is the business – that still pays
Playhouses Ball rooms – there the masquerade is
– To do what was of old – and now adays
Their maids – nay wives so innocent and blooming
Cuckold their spouses to seem honest women

167

Milton sung Eden and the fall of man
Not woman for the name implies a wh—e   10
And they would make a ruin of his plan
Falling so often they can fall no lower
Tell me a worse delusion if you can
For innoscence – and I will sing no more
Wherever mischief is tis womans brewing
Created from manself – to be mans ruin

The flower in bud hides from the fading sun
And keeps the hue of beauty on its cheek
But when full blown they into riot run
The hue turns pale and lost each ruddy streak   20
So 't'is with woman who pretends to shun
Immodest actions which they inly seek
Night hides the wh—e – cupboards tart and pasty
Flora was p—x—d – and womans quite as nasty

Marriage is nothing but a driveling hoax
To please old codgers when they're turned of forty
I wed and left my wife like other folks
But not untill I found her false and faulty
O woman fair – the man must pay thy jokes
Such makes a husband very often naughty   30
Who falls in love will seek his own undoing
The road to marriage is – 'the road to ruin'

Love worse then debt or drink or any fate
It is the damnest smart of matrimony
A hell incarnate is a woman-mate
The knot is tied – and then we loose the honey
A wife is just the protetype to hate
Commons for stock and warrens for the coney   *cattle, rabbit*
Are not more tresspassed over in rights plan
Then this incumberance on the rights of man   40

There's much said about love and more of women
I wish they were as modest as they seem

168

Some borrow husbands till their cheeks are blooming
Not like the red rose blush – but yellow cream
Lord what a while those good days are in coming –
Routs Masques and Balls – I wish they were a dream
– I wish for poor men luck – an honest praxis
Cheap food and cloathing – no corn laws or taxes

I wish – but there is little got bye wishing
I wish that bread and great coats ne'er had risen   50
I wish that there was some such word as 'pishun'
For ryhme sake for my verses must be dizen
With dresses fine – as hooks with baits for fishing
I wish all honest men were out of prison
I wish M.P's. would spin less yarn – nor doubt
But burn false bills and cross bad taxes out

I wish young married dames were not so frisky
Nor hide the ring to make believe they're single
I wish small beer was half as good as whiskey
And married dames with buggers would not mingle   60
There's some too cunning far and some too frisky
And here I want a ryhme – so write down 'jingle'
And there's such putting in – in whores crim con
Some mouths would eat forever and eat on

Childern are fond of sucking sugar candy
And maids of sausages – larger the better
Shopmen are fond of good sigars and brandy
And I of blunt – and if you change the letter
To C or K it would be quite as handy
And throw the next away – but I'm your debtor   70
For modesty – yet wishing nought between us
I'd hawl close to a she as vulcan did to venus

I really cant tell what this poem will be
About – nor yet what trade I am to follow
I thought to buy old wigs – but that will kill me

169

With cold starvation – as they're beaten hollow
Long speeches in a famine will not fill me
And madhouse traps still take me by the collar
So old wig bargains now must be forgotten
That oil that dressed them fine has made them rotten   80

I wish old wigs were done with ere they're mouldy
I wish – but heres the papers large and lusty
With speeches that full fifty times they've told ye
– Noble Lord John to sweet Miss Fanny Fusty
Is wed – a lie good reader I ne'er sold ye
– Prince Albert goes to Germany and must he
Leave the queens snuff box where all fools are strumming
From addled eggs no chickens can be coming

Whigs strum state fiddle strings untill they snap
With cuckoo cuckold cuckoo year by year   90
The razor plays it on the barbers strap
– The sissars grinder thinks it rather quere
That labour wont afford him 'one wee drap'
Of ale or gin or half and half or beer
– I wish prince Albert and the noble dastards
Who wed the wives – would get the noble bastards

I wish prince Albert on his german journey
I wish the Whigs were out of office and
Pickled in law books of some good atorney
For ways and speeches few can understand   100
They'll bless ye when in power – in prison scorn ye
And make a man rent his own house and land –
I wish prince Alberts queen was undefiled
– And every man could get his *wife* with child

I wish the devil luck with all my heart
As I would any other honest body
His bad name passes bye me like a f—t
Stinking of brimstone – then like whisky toddy

We swallow sin which seems to warm the heart
– There's no imputing any sin to God – he   110
Fills hell with work – and is'n't it a hard case
To leave old whigs and give to hell the carcass

Me—b—ne may throw his wig to little Vicky   *Lord Melbourne*
And so resign his humbug and his power
And she with the young princess mount the dickey
On ass milk diet for her german tour
Asses like ministers are rather tricky
I and the country proves it every hour
W—ll—gt—n and M—lb—n in their station   *Wellington*
Coblers to queens – are phisic to the nation   120

These batch of toadstools on this rotten tree
Shall be the cabinet of any queen
Though not such coblers as her servants be
They're of Gods making – that is plainly seen
Nor red nor green nor orange – they are free
To thrive and flourish as the Whigs have been
But come tomorrow – like the Whigs forgotten
You'll find them withered stinking dead and rotten

Death is an awfull thing it is by God
I've said so often and I think so now   130
Tis rather droll to see an old wig nod
Then doze and die the devil don't know how
Odd things are wearisome and this is odd –
Tis better work then kicking up a row   *than*
I'm weary of old Whigs and old whigs heirs
And long been sick of teazing God with prayers

I've never seen the cow turn to a bull
I've never seen the horse become an ass
I've never seen an old brawn cloathed in whool –
But I have seen full many a bonny lass   140
And wish I had one now beneath the cool

171

Of these high elms – Muse tell me where I was
O – talk of turning I've seen Whig and Tory
Turn imps of hell – and all for England's glory

I love good fellowship and wit and punning
I love 'true love' and God my taste defend
I hate most damnably all sorts of cunning –
I love the Moor and Marsh and Ponders end –
I do not like the song of 'cease your funning'
I love a modest wife and trusty friend   150
– Bricklayers want lime as I want ryhme for fillups
– So here's a health to sweet Eliza Phillips

Song

Eliza now the summer tells
Of spots where love and beauty dwells
Come and spend a day with me
Underneath the forest tree
Where the restless water flushes
Over mosses mounds and rushes
And where love and freedom dwells
With orchis flowers and fox glove bells   160
Come dear Eliza set me free
And oer the forest roam with me

Here I see the morning sun
Among the beachtree's shadows run   beech
That into gold the short sward turns
Where each bright yellow blossom burns
With hues that would his beams out shine
Yet nought can match those smiles of thine
I try to find them all the day
But none are nigh when thou'rt away   170
Though flowers bloom now on every hill
Eliza is the fairest still

172

The sun wakes up the pleasant morn
And finds me lonely and forlorn
Then wears away to sunny noon
The flowers in bloom the birds in tune
While dull and dowie all the year
No smiles to see no voice to hear
I in this forest prison lie
With none to heed my silent sigh 180
And underneath this beachen tree
With none to sigh for Love but thee

Now this new poem is entirely new
As wedding gowns or money from the mint
For all I know it is entirely true
For I would scorn to put a lie in print
– I scorn to lie for princes – so would you
And ere I shoot I try my pistol flint
– The cattle salesman – knows the way in trying
And feels his bullocks ere he thinks of buying 190

Lord bless me now the day is in the gloaming
And every evil thought is out of sight
How I should like to purchase some sweet woman
Or else creep in with my two wives to night –
Surely that wedding day is on the comeing
Abscence like phisic poisons all delight –
Mary and Martha both an evil omen
Though both my own – they still belong to no man

But to our text again – and pray where is it
Begin as parsons do at the beginning 200
Take the first line friend and you cannot miss it
'Poets are born' and so are whores for sinning
– Here's the court circular – o Lord is this it
Court cards like lists of – not the naked meaning
Here's Albert going to germany they tell us
And the young queen down in the dumps and jealous

Now you have seen a tramper on race courses
Seeking an honest penny as his trade is
Crying a list of all the running horses
And showing handbills of the sporting ladies   210
– In bills of fare you'll find a many courses
Yet all are innoscent as any maid is
Put these two dishes into one and dress it
And if there is a meaning – you may guess it

Don Juan was Ambassador from russia
But had no hand in any sort of tax
His orders hung like blossoms of the fushia
And made the ladies hearts to melt like wax
He knew Napoleon and the king of prusia
And blowed a cloud oer spirits wine or max   220
But all his profits turned out losses rather
To save one orphan which he forced to father

There's Docter Bottle imp who deals in urine
A keeper of state prisons for the queen
As great a man as is the Doge of Turin
And save in London is but seldom seen
Yclep'd old A—ll—n – mad brained ladies curing
Some p—x—d like Flora and but seldom clean
The new road oer the forest is the right one
To see red hell and further on the white one   230

Earth hells or b—gg—r sh—ps or what you please
Where men close prisoners are and women ravished
I've often seen such dirty sights as these
I've often seen good money spent and lavished
To keep bad houses up for docters fees
And I have known a b—gg—rs tally travers'd
Till all his good intents began to falter
– When death brought in his bill and left the halter

O glorious constitution what a picking
Ye've had from your tax harvest and your tythe   240

174

Old hens which cluck about that fair young chicken
– Cocks without spurs that yet can crow so blythe
Truth is shut up in prison while ye're licking
The gold from off the gingerbread – be lythe
In winding that patched broken old state clock up
Playhouses open – but mad houses lock up

Give toil more pay where rank starvation lurches
And pay your debts and put your books to rights
Leave whores and playhouses and fill your churches
Old clovenfoot your dirty victory fights   250
Like theft he still on natures manor poaches
And holds his feasting on anothers rights
To show plain truth you act in bawdy farces
Men show their tools – and maids expose their arses

Now this day is the eleventh of July
And being sunday I will seek no flaw
In man or woman – but prepare to die
In two days more I may that ticket draw
And so may thousands more as well as I
To day is here – the next who ever saw   260
And In a madhouse I can find no mirth pay
– Next tuesday used to be Lord Byrons birthday

Lord Byron poh – the man wot rites the werses
And is just what he is and nothing more
Who with his pen lies like the mist disperses
And makes all nothing as it was before
Who wed two wives and oft the truth rehearses
And might have had some twenty thousand more
Who has been dead so fools their lies are giving
And still in Allens madhouse caged and living   270

If I do wickedness to day being sunday
Can I by hearing prayers or singing psalms
Clear off all debts twixt god and man on monday

175

And lie like an old hull that dotage calms
And is there such a word as Abergundy
I've read that poem called the 'Isle of Palms'
– But singing sense pray tell me if I can
Live an old rogue and die an honest man

I wish I had a quire of foolscap paper
Hot pressed – and crowpens – how I could endite   280
A silver candlestick and green wax taper
Lord bless me what fine poems I would write
The very tailors they would read and caper
And mantua makers would be all delight
Though laurel wreaths my brows did ne'er environ
I think myself as great a bard as Byron

I have two wives and I should like to see them
Both by my side before another hour
If both are honest I should like to be them
For both are fair and bonny as a flower   290
And one o Lord – now do bring in the tea mem
Were bards pens steamers each of ten horse power
I could not bring her beautys fair to weather
So I've towed both in harbour blest together

Now i'n't this canto worth a single pound
From anybody's pocket who will buy
As thieves are worth a halter I'll be bound
Now honest reader take the book and try
And if as I have said it is not found
I'll write a better canto bye and bye   300
So reader now the money till unlock it
And buy the book and help to fill my pocket

Composed 1841   First published 1949

Age 48   JOURNEY OUT OF ESSEX

July 18 – 1841 – Sunday – Felt very melancholly – went a walk on the forest in the afternoon – fell in with some gipseys one of whom offered to assist in my escape from the mad house by hideing me in his camp to which I almost agreed but told him I had no money to start with but if he would do so I would promise him fifty pounds and he agreed to do so before saturday, on friday I went again but he did not seem so willing so I said little about it – On sunday I went and they were all gone – an old wide awake hat and an old straw bonnet of the plumb pudding sort was left behind – and I put the hat in my pocket thinking it might be usefull for another oppertunity – as good luck would have it, it turned out to be so

July 19 – Monday – Did nothing

July 20 – Reconnitered the rout the Gipsey pointed out and found it a legible one to make a movement and having only honest courage and myself in my army I Led the way and my troops soon followed but being careless in mapping down the rout as the Gipsey told me I missed the lane to Enfield town and was going down Enfield highway till I passed 'The Labour in vain' Public house where A person I knew comeing out of the door told me the way

    I walked down the lane gently and was soon in Enfield Town and bye and bye on the great York Road where it was all plain sailing and steering ahead meeting no enemy and fearing none I reached <u>Stevenage</u> where being Night I got over a gate crossed over the corner of a green paddock where seeing a pond or hollow in the corner I forced to stay off a respectable distance to keep from falling into it for my legs were nearly knocked up and began to stagger   I scaled some old rotten paleings into the yard and then had higher pailings to clamber over to get into the shed or hovel which I did with difficulty being rather weak and to my good luck I found some trusses of clover piled up about 6 or more feet square which I gladly

He went west before turning north

1st night on the road, about 25, 30 miles from Epping

10

20

30

177

mounted and slept on   there was some trays in the hovel on which I could have reposed had I not found a better bed   I slept soundly but had a very uneasy dream   I thought my first wife lay on my left arm and somebody took her away from my side which made me wake up rather unhappy   I thought as I awoke somebody said 'Mary' but nobody was near — I lay down with my head towards the north to show myself the steering point in the morning

40

2nd July 21 — [when I awoke] Daylight was looking in on every
mornng side and fearing my garrison might be taken by storm and myself be made prisoner I left my lodging by the way I got in and thanked God for his kindness in procureing it (for any thing in a famine is better then nothing and any place that giveth the weary rest is a blessing)   I gained the north road again and steered due north — on the left hand side the road under the bank like a cave I saw a Man and boy coiled up asleep which I hailed and they woke up to tell me the name of the next village

50

Some where on the London side the 'Plough' Public house a Man passed me on horseback in a Slop frock and said 'here's another of the broken down haymakers' and threw me a penny to get a half pint of beer which I picked up and thanked him for and when I got to the plough I called for a half pint and drank it and got a rest and escaped a very heavy shower in the bargain by having a shelter till it was over — afterwards I would have begged a penny of two drovers who were very saucey so I begged no more of any body meet who I would

60

— I passed 3 or 4 good built houses on a hill and a public house on the road side in the hollow below them   I seemed to pass the Milestones very quick in the morning but towards night they seemed to be stretched further asunder   I got to a village further on and forgot the name   the road on the left hand was quite over shaded by some trees and quite dry so I sat down half an hour and made a good many wishes for breakfast but wishes was no hearty meal so I got up as hungry as I sat down — I forget here the names of the villages I passed through but reccolect at

late evening going through <u>Potton</u> in Bedfordshire where I
called in a house to light my pipe in which was a civil old
woman and a young country wench makeing lace on a cushion
as round as a globe and a young fellow all civil people – I asked
them a few questions as to the way and where the clergyman
and overseer lived but they scarcely heard me or gave me no
answer

    I then went through Potton and happened with a kind
talking country man who told me the Parson lived a good way
from where I was or overseer I do'n't know which so I went on
hopping with a crippled foot for the gravel had got into my old
shoes one of which I had now nearly lost the sole   Had I found
the overseers house at hand or the Parsons I should have gave
my name and begged for a shilling to carry me home but I was
forced to brush on pennyless and be thankfull I had a leg to
move on – I then asked him wether he could tell me of a farm
yard any where on the road where I could find a shed and some
dry straw and he said yes and if you will go with me I will show
you the place – its a public house on the left hand side the road at
the sign of the 'Ram' but seeing a stone or flint heap I longed to
rest as one of my feet was very painfull so I thanked him for his
kindness and bid him go on – but the good natured fellow
lingered awhile as if wishing to conduct me and then suddenly
reccolecting that he had a hamper on his shoulder and a lock up
bag in his hand cram full to meet the coach which he feared
missing – he started hastily and was soon out of sight – I
followed looking in vain for the country mans straw bed – and
not being able to meet it I lay down by a shed side under some
Elm trees between the wall and the trees being a thick row
planted some 5 or 6 feet from the buildings   I lay there and
tried to sleep but the wind came in between them so cold that I
lay till I quaked like the ague and quitted the lodging for a better
at the Ram which I could hardly hope to find – It now began to
grow dark apace and the odd houses on the road began to light
up and show the inside tennants' lots very comfortable and my
outside lot very uncomfortable and wretched – still I hobbled
forward as well as I could and at last came to the Ram   the

[margin notes:]
70 About 16 miles from Stevenage
80
90
100
2nd night

shutters were not closed and the lighted window looked very cheering but I had no money and did not like to go in there was a sort of shed or gighouse at the end but I did not like to lie there as the people were up – so I still travelled on the road 110 was very lonely and dark in places being overshaded with trees at length I came to a place where the road branched off into two turnpikes one to the right about and the other straight forward and on going bye my eye glanced on a mile stone standing under the hedge so I heedlessly turned back to read it to see where the other road led too and on doing so I found it led to London I then suddenly forgot which was North or South and though I narrowly examined both ways I could see no tree or bush or stone heap that I could reccolect I had passed so I went on mile after mile almost convinced I was going the 120 same way I came and these thoughts were so strong upon me that doubt and hopelessness made me turn so feeble that I was scarcely able to walk yet I could not sit down or give up but shuffled along till I saw a lamp shining as bright as the moon which on nearing I found was suspended over a Tollgate before I got through the man came out with a candle and eyed me narrowly but having no fear I stopt to ask him wether I was going northward and he said when you get through the gate you are; so I thanked him kindly and went through on the other side and gathered my old strength as my 130 doubts vanished I soon cheered up and hummed the air of highland Mary as I went on I at length fell in with an odd house all alone near a wood but I could not see what the sign was though the sign seemed to stand oddly enough in a sort of trough or spout there was a large porch over the door and being weary I crept in and glad enough I was to find I could lye with my legs straight the inmates were all gone to roost for I could hear them turn over in bed as I lay at full length on the stones in the poach – I slept here till daylight and felt very much refreshed as I got up – I blest my two wives and both their familys when I 140 lay down and when I got up and when I thought of some former difficultys on a like occasion I could not help blessing the Queen Having passed a Lodge on the left hand within a mile

July 22,
3rd
morning

and half or less of a town I think it might be St Ives but I forget
the name I sat down to rest on a flint heap where I might rest
half an hour or more and while sitting here I saw a tall Gipsey
come out of the Lodge gate and make down the road towards
where I was sitting   when she got up to me on seeing she was a
young woman with an honest looking countenance rather
handsome I spoke to her and asked her a few questions which   150
she answered readily and with evident good humour so I got up
and went on to the next town with her – she cautioned me on
the way to put somthing in my hat to keep the crown up and
said in a lower tone 'you'll be noticed' but not knowing what
she hinted – I took no notice and made no reply   at length she
pointed to a small tower church which she called Shefford
Church and advised me to go on a footway which would take
me direct to it and I should shorten my journey fifteen miles by
doing so   I would gladly have taken the young woman's advice
feeling that it was honest and a nigh guess towards the truth but   160
fearing I might loose my way and not be able to find the north
road again I thanked her and told her I should keep to the road
when she bade me 'good day' and went into a house or shop on
the left hand side the road   I have but a slight reccolection of
my journey between here and Stilton for I was knocked up and
noticed little or nothing – one night I lay in a dyke bottom from **3rd night?**
the wind and went sleep half an hour when I suddenly awoke
and found one side wet through from the sock in the dyke
bottom so I got out and went on – I remember going down a
very dark road hung over with trees on both sides very thick   170
which seemed to extend a mile or two   I then entered a town
and some of the chamber windows had candle lights shineing in
them – I felt so weak here that I forced to sit down on the
ground to rest myself and while I sat here a Coach that seemed
to be heavy laden came rattling up and stopt in the hollow
below me and I cannot reccolect its ever passing by me   I then
got up and pushed onward seeing little to notice for the road
very often looked as stupid as myself and I was very often half
asleep as I went   on the <u>third</u> day I satisfied my hunger by eat-   **fourth?,**
ing the grass by the road side which seemed to taste something   180 **or perhaps he 181 is thinking back to the 3rd day.**

like bread   I was hungry and eat heartily till I was satisfied and in fact the meal seemed to do me good   the next and last day I reccollected that I had some tobacco and my box of lucifers being exausted I could not light my pipe so I took to chewing Tobacco all day and eat the quids when I had done and I was never hungry afterwards – I remember passing through Buckden and going a length of road afterwards but I dont reccolect the name of any place untill I came to stilton where I was compleatly foot foundered and broken down   when I had got about half through the town a gravel causeway invited me to rest myself so I lay down and nearly went sleep   a young woman (so I guessed by the voice) came out of a house and said 'poor creature' and another more elderly said 'O he shams' but when I got up the latter said 'o no he don't' as I hobbled along very lame   I heard the voices but never looked back to see where they came from – when I got near the Inn at the end of the gravel walk I met two young women and I asked one of them wether the road branching to the right bye the end of the Inn did not lead to Peterborough and she said 'Yes' it did so as soon as ever I was on it I felt myself in homes way and went on rather more cheerfull though I forced to rest oftener then usual   before I got to Peterborough a man and woman passed me in a cart and on hailing me as they passed I found they were neighbours from Helpstone where I used to live – I told them I was knocked up which they could easily see and that I had neither eat or drank any thing since I left Essex   when I told my story they clubbed together and threw me fivepence out of the cart   I picked it up and called at a small public house near the bridge were I had two half pints of ale and twopenn'oth of bread and cheese   when I had done I started quite refreshed only my feet was more crippled then ever and I could scarcely make a walk of it over the stones and being half ashamed to sit down in the street I forced to keep on the move and got through Peterborough better then I expected   when I got on the high road I rested on the stone heaps as I passed till I was able to go on afresh and bye and bye I passed Walton and soon reached Werrington and was making for the Beehive as fast as I could

July 23
4th day

about
24 miles
north of
190 Potto.

200

210

about
7 miles
beyond
Stilton

Clare had walked about 80 miles in four days.

when a cart met me with a man and woman and a boy in it when
nearing me the woman jumped out and caught fast hold of my
hands and wished me to get into the cart but I refused and   220
thought her either drunk or mad but when I was told it was my
second wife Patty I got in and was soon at Northborough   but
Mary was not there neither could I get any information about
her further then the old story of her being dead six years ago   *than*
which might be taken from a bran new old Newspaper printed a
dozen years ago but I took no notice of the blarney having seen
her myself about a twelvemonth ago alive and well and as
young as ever – so here I am homeless at home and half gratified
to feel that I can be happy anywhere

    'May none those marks of my sad fate efface   230
    'For they appeal from tyranny to God'
                         Byron

July 24th 1841 Returned home out of Essex and found no Mary
– her and her family are as nothing to me now though she
herself was once the dearest of all – and how can I forget [. . .]

Composed 1841   *First published 1865*   *Mary Joyce had actually died in 1838 Clare's stay at home lasted 5 months before he was recommitted to an asylum.*

from CHILD HAROLD

Many are poets – though they use no pen
To show their labours to the shuffling age
Real poets must be truly honest men
Tied to no mongrel laws on flattery's page
No zeal have they for wrong or party rage
– The life of labour is a rural song
That hurts no cause – nor warfare tries to wage
Toil like the brook in music wears along –
Great little minds claim right to act the wrong   9
        [. . .]

My life hath been one love – no blot it out
My life hath been one chain of contradictions

Madhouses Prisons wh—re shops – never doubt
But that my life hath had some strong convictions
That such was wrong – religion makes restrictions
I would have followed – but life turned a bubble   150
And clumb the jiant stile of maledictions
They took me from my wife and to save trouble
I wed again and made the error double

Yet abscence claims them both and keeps them too
And locks me in a shop in spite of law
Among a low lived set and dirty crew
Here let the Muse oblivions curtain draw
And let man think – for God hath often saw
Things here too dirty for the light of day
For in a madhouse there exists no law –   160
Now stagnant grows my too refined clay
I envy birds their wings to flye away

How servile is the task to please alone
Though beauty woo and love inspire the song
Mere painted beauty with her heart of stone
Thinks the world worships while she flaunts along
The flower of sunshine butterflye of song
Give me the truth of heart in womans life
The love to cherish one – and do no wrong
To none – O peace of every care and strife   170
Is true love in an estimable wife

How beautifull this hill of fern swells on
So beautifull the chappel peeps between
The hornbeams – with its simple bell – alone
I wander here hid in a palace green
Mary is abscent – but the forest queen
Nature is with me – morning noon and gloaming
I write my poems in these paths unseen
And when among these brakes and beeches roaming
I sigh for truth and home and love and woman   180

184

I sigh for one and two – and still I sigh
For many are the whispers I have heard
From beauty's lips – loves soul in many an eye
Hath pierced my heart with such intense regard
I Looked for joy and pain was the reward
I think of them I love each girl and boy
Babes of two mothers – on this velvet sward
And nature thinks – in her so sweet employ
While dews fall on each blossom weeping joy

Here is the chappel yard enclosed with pales   190
And oak trees nearly top its little bell
Here is the little bridge with guiding rail
That leads me on to many a pleasant dell
The fernowl chitters like a startled knell
To nature – yet tis sweet at evening still –
A pleasant road curves round the gentle swell
Where nature seems to have her own sweet will
Planting her beech and thorn about the sweet fern hill

I have had many loves – and seek no more –
These solitudes my last delights shall be   200
The leaf hid forest – and the lonely shore
Seem to my mind like beings that are free
Yet would I had some eye to smile on me
Some heart where I could make a happy home in
Sweet Susan that was wont my love to be
And Bessey of the glen – for I've been roaming
With both at morn and noon and dusky gloaming

Cares gather round I snap their chains in two
And smile in agony and laugh in tears
Like playing with a deadly serpent – who   210
Stings to the death – there is no room for fears
Where death would bring me happiness – his sheers
Kills cares that hiss to poison many a vein
The thought to be extinct my fate endears

Pale death the grand phisician cures all pain
The dead rest well – who lived for joys in vain
      [. . .]

Tis pleasant now day's hours begin to pass
To dewy Eve – To walk down narrow close
And feel one's feet among refreshing grass
And hear the insects in their homes discourse   420
And startled blackbird flye from covert close
Of white thorn hedge with wild fear's fluttering wings
And see the spire and hear the clock toll hoarse
And whisper names – and think oer many things
That love hurds up in truth's imaginings   *hoards*

Fame blazed upon me like a comet's glare
Fame waned and left me like a fallen star
Because I told the evil what they are
And truth and falshood never wished to mar
My Life hath been a wreck – and I've gone far   430
For peace and truth – and hope – for home and rest
– Like Eden's gates – fate throws a constant bar –
Thoughts may o'ertake the sunset in the west
– Man meets no home within a woman's breast

Though they are blazoned in the poet's song
As all the comforts which our lifes contain
I read and sought such joys my whole life long
And found the best of poets sung in vain
But still I read and sighed and sued again
And lost no purpose where I had the will   440
I almost worshiped when my toils grew vain
Finding no antidote my pains to kill
I sigh a poet and a lover still
      [. . .]

Sweet comes the misty mornings in september
Among the dewy paths how sweet to stray

Greensward or stubbles as I well remember
I once have done – the mist curls thick and grey
As cottage smoke – like net work on the sprey   700
Or seeded grass the cobweb draperies run
Beaded with pearls of dew at early day
And oer the pleachy stubbles peeps the sun   *bleached*
The lamp of day when that of night is done

What mellowness these harvest days unfold
In the strong glances of the midday sun
The homesteads very grass seems changed to gold
The light in golden shadows seems to run
And tinges every spray it rests upon
With that rich harvest hue of sunny joy   710
Nature lifes sweet companion cheers alone –
The hare starts up before the shepherd boy
And partridge coveys wir on russet wings of joy   *whir*

The meadow flags now rustle bleached and dank
And misted oer with down as fine as dew
The sloe and dewberry shine along the bank
Where weeds in blooms luxuriance lately grew
Red rose the sun and up the morehen flew
From bank to bank the meadow arches stride
Where foamy floods in winter tumbles through   720
And spread a restless ocean foaming wide
Where now the cowboys sleep nor fear the coming tide

About the medows now I love to sit
On banks bridge walls and rails as when a boy
To see old trees bend oer the flaggy pit
With hugh roots bare that time does not destroy
Where sits the angler at his days employ
And there Ivy leaves the bank to climb
The tree – and now how sweet to weary joy
– Aye nothing seems so happy and sublime   730
As sabbath bells and their delightfull chime

187

Sweet solitude thou partner of my life
Thou balm of hope and every pressing care
Thou soothing silence oer the noise of strife
These meadow flats and trees – the Autumn air
Mellows my heart to harmony – I bear
Life's burthen happily – these fenny dells
Seem Eden in this sabbath rest from care
My heart with love's first early memory swells
To hear the music of those village bells   740

For in that hamlet lives my rising sun
Whose beams hath cheered me all my lorn life long
My heart to nature there was early won
For she was nature's self – and still my song
Is her through sun and shade through right and wrong
On her my memory forever dwells
The flower of Eden – evergreen of song
Truth in my heart the same love story tells
– I love the music of those village bells

Composed 1841   First published 1949

TIS <u>MARTINMAS</u> FROM RIG   *St. Martin's Day, Nov. 11*
TO RIG

Tis martinmass from rig to rig
Ploughed fields and meadow lands are <u>blea</u>   *bleak*
In hedge and field each restless twig
Is dancing on the naked tree
Flags in the dykes are bleached and brown
Docks by its sides are dry and dead
All but the ivy bows are brown
Upon each leaning dotterels head

Crimsoned with <u>awes</u> the awthorns bend   *hawes*
Oer meadow dykes and rising floods   10

The wild geese seek the reedy fen
And dark the storm comes oer the woods
The crowds of lapwings load the air
With buzes of a thousand wings
There flocks of <u>starnels</u> too repair   *starlings*
When morning oer the valley springs

Composed 1841   First published 1935

LORD HEAR MY PRAYER
WHEN TROUBLE GLOOMS

Paraphrase of Psalm 102

Lord hear my prayer when trouble glooms
Let sorrow find a way
And when the day of trouble comes
Turn not thy face away
My bones like hearth stones burn away
My life like vapoury smoke decays

My heart is smitten like the grass
That withered lies and dead
And I so lost to what I was
Forget to eat my bread   10
My voice is groaning all the day
My bones prick through this skin of clay

The wildernesses pelican
The deserts lonely owl
I am their like a desert man
In ways as lone and foul
As sparrows on the cottage top
I wait till I with faintness drop

I bear my enemies reproach
All silently I mourn   20
They on my private peace encroach
Against me they are sworn

189

Ashes as bread my trouble shares
And mix my food with weeping cares

Yet not for them is sorrows toil
I fear no mortals frown
But thou hast held me up awhile
And thou hast cast me down
My days like shadows waste from view
I mourn like withered grass in dew   30

But thou Lord shalt endure forever
All generations through
Thou shalt to Zion be the giver
Of joy and mercey too
Her very stones are in their trust
Thy servants reverence her dust

Heathens shall hear and fear thy name
All kings of earth thy glory know
When thou shalt build up Zions fame   40
And live in glory there below
He'll not despise their prayers though mute
But still regard the destitute

Composed 1841   First published 1949

MARY

1

It is the evening hour,
How silent all doth lie,
The hornèd moon she shows her face,
In the river, with the sky;
Just by the path on which we pass,
The flaggy lake, lies still, as glass.

2

Spirit of her I love,
Wispering to me:
Stories of sweet visions, as I rove:
Here stop and crop with me,   10
Sweet flowers, that in the still hour grew,
We'll take them home, nor shake off the bright dew.

3

Mary, or sweet spirit of thee,
As the bright sun shines tomorrow;
Thy dark eyes these flowers shall see,
Gathered by me in sorrow,
In the still hour, when my mind was free,
To walk alone – yet wish I walk'd with thee.

Composed early 1840s   *First published 1924*

[handwritten annotation: conflict between scansion and rhyme]

[handwritten annotation: In contrast to his usual lack of punctuation, here Clare has too much.]

SONG

A seaboy on the giddy mast
Sees nought but ocean waves
And hears the wild inconstant blast
Where loud the tempest raves

My life is like the ocean wave
And like the inconstant sea
In every hope appears a grave
And leaves no hope for me

My life is like the ocean's lot
Bright gleams the morning gave   10
But storms oerwhelmed the sunny spot
Deep in the ocean wave

My life hath been the ocean storm
A black and troubled sea
When shall I find my life a calm
A port and harbour free

Composed 1843   First published 1949

SONG LAST DAY

There is a day a dreadfull day
Still following the past
When sun and moon are past away
And mingle with the blast
There is a vision in my eye
A vacuum o'er my mind
Sometimes as on the sea I lye
Mid roaring waves and wind

When valleys rise to mountain waves
And mountains sink to seas   10
When towns and cities temples graves
All vanish like a breeze
The skyes that was are past and o'er
That almanack of days
Year chronicles are kept no more
Oblivions ruin pays

Pays in destruction shades and hell
Sin goes in darkness down
And therein sulphurs shadows dwell
Worth wins and wears the crown   20
The very shore if shore I see
All shrivelled to a scroll
The Heaven's rend away from me
And thunders sulphurs roll

192

Black as the deadly thunder cloud
The stars shall turn to dun
And heaven by that darkness bowed
Shall make days light be done
When stars and skys shall all decay
And earth no more shall be   30
When heaven itself shall pass away
Then thou'lt remember me

Composed c. 1845   First published 1964

LOOK THROUGH THE NAKED
BRAMBLE AND BLACK THORN

Look through the naked bramble and black thorn
And see the arum show its vivid green
Glossy and rich and some ink spotted like the morn—
Ing sky with clouds – in sweetest neuks I've been   *nooks*
And seen the arum sprout its happy green
Full of spring visions and green thoughts o' may
Dead leaves a' litter where its leaves are seen
Broader and brighter green from day to day
Beneath the hedges in their leafless spray

Composed c. 1845   First published 1964

I AM

1

I am – yet what I am, none cares or knows;
   My friends forsake me like a memory lost: –
I am the self-consumer of my woes; –
   They rise and vanish in oblivion's host,
Like shadows in love's frenzied stifled throes: –
And yet I am, and live – like vapours tost *(tossed)*

2

Into the nothingness of scorn and noise, –
   Into the living sea of waking dreams,
Where there is neither sense of life or joys,
   But the vast shipwreck of my lifes esteems;   10
Even the dearest, that I love the best
Are strange – nay, rather stranger than the rest.

3

I long for scenes, where man hath never trod
   A place where woman never smiled or wept
There to abide with my Creator, God;
   And sleep as I in childhood, sweetly slept,
Untroubling, and untroubled where I lie,
The grass below – above the vaulted sky.

Composed 1840s   First published 1848

THE CROW

How peaceable it seems for lonely men
To see a crow fly in the thin blue sky
Over the woods and feals, o'er level fen
It speaks of villages, or cottage nigh
Behind the neighbouring woods – when march winds high
Tear off the branches of the hugh old oak
I love to see these chimney sweeps sail by
And hear them o'er the knarled forest croak
Then <u>sosh</u> askew from the hid woodmans stroke   *swoop*
That in the woods their daily labours ply   10
I love the sooty crow nor would provoke
Its march day exercises of croaking joy
I love to see it sailing to and fro
While feals, and woods and waters spread below

Composed 1840s   First published 1924

194

THERE IS A CHARM IN
SOLITUDE THAT CHEERS

There is a charm in Solitude that cheers
A feeling that the world knows nothing of
A green delight the wounded mind endears
After the hustling world is broken off
Whose whole delight was crime at good to scoff
Green solitude his prison pleasure yields
The bitch fox heeds him not – birds seem to laugh
He lives the Crusoe of his lonely fields
Which dark green oaks his noontide leisure shields

Composed before 1856   First published 1949

THE PEASANT POET

He loved the brook's soft sound
The swallow swimming by
He loved the daisy covered ground
The cloud bedappled sky
To him the dismal storm appeared
The very voice of God
And where the Evening rock was reared
Stood Moses with his rod

And every thing his eyes surveyed
The insects I' the brake   bracken   10
Where Creatures God almighty made
He loved them for his sake
A silent man in life's affairs
A thinker from a Boy
A Peasant in his daily cares –
The Poet in his joy

Composed before 1856   First published 1920

Cowper the Poet of the field
   Who found the muse on common ground
The homesteads that each Cottage shields
   He loved and made them Classic ground

The lonely house the rural walk
   He sang so musically true
E'en now they share the peoples talk
   Who love the poet Cowper too

Who has not read the 'Winter storm'
   And does not feel the fallen snow   10
And Woodmen keeping noses warm
   With pipes where ever Forests grow

In France in Germany and Spain
   The same delightful pictures show
The Cowpers 'Woodmens' seen again
   And Lurchers tracking thro the snow

The 'Winters walk' and 'Summers Noon'
   We meet together by the fire
And think the 'walks' are o'er too soon
   When books are read and we retire   20

Who travels o'er those sweet fields now
   And brings not Cowper to his mind
Birds sing his name on every bough
   Nature repeats it in the wind

And every place the Poet trod
   And every place the Poet sung
Are like the holy land of God
   In every Mouth on every tongue

Composed before 1856   First published 1935

THE WINTERS COME

1

Sweet chesnuts brown, like soleing leather turn,
The larch trees, like the colour of the sun,
That paled sky in the Autumn seem'd to burn.
What a strange scene before us now does run,
Red, brown, and yellow, russet black, and dun,
White thorn, wild cherry, and the poplar bare,
The sycamore all withered in the sun,
No leaves are now upon the birch tree there,
All now is stript to the cold wintry air.

2

See! not one tree but what has lost its leaves,   10
And yet, the landscape wears a pleasing hue,
The winter chill on his cold bed receives,
Foliage which once hung oer the waters blue,
Naked, and bare, the leafless trees repose,
Blue headed titmouse now seeks maggots rare,
Sluggish, and dull, the leaf strewn river flows,
That is not green, which was so through the year,
Dark chill November draweth to a close.

3

'Tis winter! and I love to read in-doors,
When the moon hangs her crescent upon high: 20
While on the window shutters the wind roars,
And storms like furies pass remorseless by,
How pleasant on a feather bed to lie,
Or sitting by the fire, in fancy soar,
With Milton, or with Dante to regions high,
Or read fresh volumes we've not seen before,
Or o'er old Bartons 'melancholy' pore.

Burton's 'Anatomy of Melancholy'

Composed before 1856   First published 1920

197

FRAGMENT

The Elm tree's heavy foliage meets the eye
Propt in dark masses on the evening sky
The lighter ash but half obstructs the view
Leaving grey openings where the light looks through

Composed before 1856   First published 1949

TO JOHN CLARE

Well honest John how fare you now at home
The spring is come and birds are building nests
The old cock robin to the stye is come
With olive feathers and its ruddy breast
And the old cock with wattles and red comb
Struts with the hens and seems to like some best
Then crows and looks about for little crumbs
Swept out bye little folks an hour ago
The pigs sleep in the sty the bookman comes
The little boys lets home close nesting go   10
And pockets tops and tawes where daiseys bloom
To look at the new number just laid down   *a sixpenny roman*
With lots of pictures and good stories too
And Jack the jiant killers high renown

Composed 1860   First published 1861

198

LETTER TO JAMES HIPKINS

March 8 1860

DEAR SIR

I am in a Madhouse and quite forget your Name or who you are
You must excuse me for I have nothing to communicate or tell
of and why I am shut up I dont know I have nothing to
say so I conclude

Yours respectfully
JOHN CLARE

Composed 1860   First published 1951

BIRDS NESTS

Tis Spring warm glows the South
Chaffinchs carry the moss in his mouth
To the filbert hedges all day long
And charms the poet with his beautifull song
The wind blows <u>blea</u> oer the sedgey fen   bleak
But warm the sunshines by the little wood
Where the old Cow at her leisure chews her cud

Composed 1863–4   First published 1864

Clare's last poem, written a few
months before he died. How
appropriate that it is about birds'
nests. As Edward Thomas says,
"He is the best of all poets at suggesting
the nests and eggs of wild birds." Not
the greatest of praises, perhaps, but
still not entirely trivial.

Critical commentary

First, a piece of practical criticism. Compare and contrast Wordsworth's poem 'Gipsies' (1807) with John Clare's 'The gipsy camp',
written some thirty years later. Wordsworth's poem comes first:

Yet are they here the same unbroken knot
Of human Beings, in the self-same spot!
Men, women, children, yea the frame
Of the whole spectacle the same!
Only their fire seems bolder, yielding light,
Now deep and red, the colouring of night;
That on their Gipsy-faces falls,
Their bed of straw and blanket-walls.
Twelve hours, twelve bounteous hours, are gone, while I
Have been a traveller under open sky,
Much witnessing of change and cheer,
Yet as I left I find them here!
The weary Sun betook himself to rest; –
Then issued Vesper from the fulgent west,
Outshining like a visible God
The glorious path in which he trod.
And now, ascending, after one dark hour
And one night's diminution of her power,
Behold the mighty Moon! this way

*The moon has risen an hour after
dark has fallen, so the moon is
a day or so past full and is in
its waning phase.*

201

She looks as if at them – but they
Regard not her: – oh better wrong and strife
(By nature transient) than this torpid life;
Life which the very stars reprove
As on their silent tasks they move!
Yet witness all that stirs in heaven or earth!
In scorn I speak not; – they are what their birth
And breeding suffer them to be;
Wild outcasts of society!

In complete contrast, here is Clare's:

The snow falls deep; the Forest lies alone:
The boy goes hasty for his load of <u>brakes</u>,
Then thinks upon the fire and hurries back;
The Gipsy knocks his hands and tucks them up,
And seeks his squalid camp, half hid in snow,
Beneath the oak, which breaks away the wind,
And bushes close, with snow like hovel warm:
There <u>stinking</u> mutton roasts upon the coals,
And the half-roasted dog squats close and rubs,
Then feels the heat too strong and goes aloof;
He watches well, but none a bit can spare,
And vainly waits the morsel thrown away:
'Tis thus they live – a picture to the place;
A quiet, pilfering, unprotected race.

[margin note, handwritten:] bracken, for kindli or for a windbr or bedding

[margin note, handwritten:] probably carrion; at best, not freshly killed; however pilferi the gypsies wou not have dared kill a farmer's sheep.

Many students will have had their first encounter with Clare in
some such way. If the poets' names are on the paper, they may well
assume that Wordsworth was a great poet while Clare was not, and
react accordingly. But if we ignore the names and concentrate on the
poems, it will be obvious that the second is far better. Wordsworth
in 'Gipsies' is at his most bombastic (the poem is studded all over
with exclamation marks); the images ('Vesper' and 'the mighty
Moon') are tired, and he is clearly not writing about the gipsies
themselves but about his own reactions to them, based on two brief
sightings from horseback. And he is over-reacting, working himself
up into a lather of false emotion because they have not yet moved on,

and do not look at the moon. Clare's poem impresses by its quiet objectivity. He does not moralize about the gipsies, whom he evidently knows quite well; what he does is to build up a detailed picture of their rather squalid way of life, with the cold and the bad food which they endure passively, and then puts it into perspective. That last line, which balances their negative qualities – 'pilfering' – against the fact that they are quiet and unprotected, is beautifully judged. Certainly no one reading this sober and compassionate poem without previous knowledge would have guessed that the author was mad. *A "beautifully judged" evaluation, as well as a beautifully judged poem.*

A NORTHAMPTONSHIRE PEASANT

'Poems Descriptive of Rural Life and Scenery, by John Clare, a Northamptonshire Peasant', was the title-page of Clare's first book. It may seem unusual to typecast a writer in this way, and the implication is that the poems would not have been worth printing if Clare had not been a Northamptonshire peasant. 'It is not done well', as Dr Johnson said of women preachers, 'but you are ✳ surprised to find it done at all.' The standard Victorian attitude to Clare was expressed by Leslie Stephen in the *Dictionary of National Biography*:

Though Clare shows fine natural taste, and has many exquisite descriptive touches, his poetry does not rise to a really high level; and, though extraordinary under the circumstances, requires for its appreciation that the circumstances should be remembered.

That was written a hundred years ago, but Clare still has not achieved the status of a major poet. It is quite possible to take a degree in English literature without knowing any of his work except a few anthology pieces ('I am', or 'Little Trotty Wagtail', on their very different levels). He is much less famous than his contemporaries Keats and Shelley, although he left a far larger body of good work. But his popularity is growing – especially among ordinary readers – and more and more critics are beginning to insist that he deserves a very high place. As Geoffrey Grigson wrote, as long ago as

203

✳ The punch line to the joke that begins: How is a woman preacher like a dog walking on its hind legs?

a word that Clare would have scoffed at, and rightly so!

1949, 'Clare has gradually been transformed from "peasant-poet" into poet, from cottage rushlight into what indeed he is, a star of considerable and most unique <u>coruscation</u>.'

There are several reasons why the process has taken so long. Many of his best poems were not published until well into the twentieth century; at the time of writing, there is still no complete edition. There are special difficulties – his use of dialect words, his odd spelling and lack of punctuation – which may discourage casual readers. And perhaps some still feel that, after all, he was only a Northamptonshire peasant. He had the minimum of formal education; he never left England and did not often travel far from his birthplace in the East Midlands; he died in a lunatic asylum. It is tempting to say that his life was more extraordinary than his work.

Readers will draw their own conclusions from this volume, which is a selection of what we believe to be Clare's best poems (he wrote a very large number, many of them second-rate). We have omitted most of the love poems, except <u>'Mary', one of the greatest lyrics in the language</u>. Several 'mad' poems are included (among them the whole of 'Don Juan', not a good work in itself) because they show, with great intensity, what was happening to Clare's mind as it broke up. But we have concentrated on the 'poems descriptive of rural life and scenery' – that is, poems about the little-known country on the edge of the Fens; its birds, animals, weather and people. There is also a fairly large selection of work other than poetry, although his first biographer, Frederick W. Martin, stated in 1865 that there was 'no doubt whatever of the absolute incapacity of [Clare] to write prose'. In fact the prose has a great deal to offer – an invaluable account of the poet's early life, absorbing descriptions of nature, and of course the 'Journey out of Essex', one of those pieces which could not possibly be left out of any Clare anthology. 'Returned home out of Essex and found no Mary' – whether or not we know the full story, we can still feel the pain behind the few bald words.

Even in the 1980s, editing Clare presents special problems. We have decided not to modernize his spelling or to insert punctuation. 'I am generally understood', he observed, 'tho I do not use that awkward squad of pointing called commas colons semicolons etc.' His manuscripts – which can be seen at Northampton and

Peterborough – are not easy to read, and his first editors and publishers often produced inaccurate texts. The real work of editing began in the mid-twentieth century, when Eric Robinson and his colleagues published the majority of his poems in the form in which he wrote them. 'Once the business of correction is begun, there is no end', they wrote, 'and the editor soon finds himself trying to rewrite Clare's verse for him' (Eric Robinson and Geoffrey Summerfield, Introduction to *Selected Poems and Prose of John Clare*, Oxford 1967). Wherever possible, we have relied on these indispensable editions.

A stumbling-block for some people is Clare's use of the Northamptonshire dialect, which was still being spoken in the East Midlands long after he died. 'I was fascinated' (a friend wrote) 'to find in his poems dialect words that my father used to use quite regularly, as well as *his* father, who was born in 1869.' Thomas Hardy, who had probably not read Clare but who was concerned about the disappearance of regional dialects, wrote in 1908:

> Education in the west of England as elsewhere has gone on with its silent and inevitable effacements, reducing the speech of this country to uniformity, and obliterating every year many a fine old local word. The process is always the same: the word is ridiculed by the newly taught; it gets into disgrace; it is heard in holes and corners only; it dies; and, worst of all, it leaves no synonym.

With the coming of radio and television, this process has been greatly speeded up, and many of Clare's local words – 'as common around me as the grass under my feet' – are now extinct. For most of them, there *is* no synonym. One example is 'crizzle', a word which describes the process by which water begins to crystallize or freeze – 'And the white frost gins crizzle pond and brook' ('The woodman'). Or if we take the line

Drowking lies the meadow-sweet ('Noon')

and substitute 'drooping', we lose the overtones of 'drought' and 'drowning' which give such a vivid impression of the flower perishing out of its natural element. Again, most readers would not want to lose the image of the bird which 'suthied up and flew against the wind' ('Wild duck's nest'), even if they did not know that the verb 'suther' means to make a sighing or rushing sound. As a matter of fact Clare uses dialect quite sparingly, especially in his later poems. Readers can understand them easily enough with the help of a glossary, and the rewards are exceptionally rich.

Few people have ever complained of not understanding Clare's poetry. Apart from the dialect words, his language is extremely simple; for much of the time he wrote as he spoke: 'Well I declare it is the pettichaps' ('The pettichaps nest'). If anything, he is too accessible to be fully valued in an age when, according to T. S. Eliot, poetry 'must be *difficult*'. Consider these lines from 'Noon', written when he was about 16:

Ragged-robbins once so pink
Now are turn'd as black as ink,
And their leaves being scorch'd so much
Even crumble at the touch.

Nothing could be simpler. Yet it is hard to say how it could have been done better; just as we feel that we thoroughly know the gipsies after having read Clare's description of them, so these four short lines give us the sense that we can actually see and touch the ragged robins.

Clare, as we have said, had had some formal education, and as an adult he read a great deal of poetry: Shakespeare and the Elizabethans including Donne, the Augustans, the much underrated Chatterton, the older and younger Romantics. He could hardly avoid being influenced by them to some extent, and there were plenty of people eager to give this ignorant 'peasant' good advice. His publisher told him that instead of using 'the language of common everyday Description' he should 'raise your Views generally, and speak of the Appearances of Nature each month more philosophically'. So we often find, at the beginning of his writing career, that he had his eye on literary models. Some pieces clearly show the influence of eighteenth-century masters such as Goldsmith or Gray. A labourer may be described as a 'swain', or by the abstract noun 'labour'; children are 'love's sweet pledges'; a cottage a 'cot';

grass 'velvet sward' and so on. Even the best of his early poems are full of such examples:

> And as most lab'rers knowingly pretend
> By certain signs to judge the weather right
> As oft from 'noahs ark' great floods desend
> And 'burred moons' fortell great storms at night
> In such like things the wood man took delight
> And ere he went to bed woud always ken
> Wether the sky was gloomd or stars shone bright
> Then went to comforts arms till morn and then
> As cheery as the sunrise beams resumd his toils agen
>
> ('The woodman')

The first lines show Clare at the peak of his powers, the exact observer of the labourers' traditions and weather lore, and the master of language. But when he describes sleep as 'comforts arms', and claims that the woodman is 'as cheery as the sunrise beams' (although the poem has already made it clear that getting up at 4 a.m. on a winter morning is not pleasant), he is much less convincing. (Perhaps he kept stressing that the woodman was pious and contented with his lot because that was what his London readers wanted to hear.) Even when he was a fairly mature and experienced artist he continued to turn out poems with titles like 'On seeing the cast and bust of the Princess Victoria', or 'Beauty's decay', of which no more need be said.

Nevertheless Clare was continually trying to purify his language, to bring it closer to what Wordsworth called 'the real language of men'. He tried out his first poems on his parents and found

> their remarks was very useful to me. At some things they woud laugh, here I distinguished affectation and conceit from nature. Some verses they woud desire me to repeat again, as they said they could not understand them; here I discover'd obscurity from common sense, and always benefited by making it as much like the latter as I could; for I thought if they could not understand me, my taste should be wrong founded, and not agreeable to nature.

207

Perhaps this gives a clue to why, with all his disadvantages, he is such a great poet.

In the first place, he had that way with words which seems to be a gift independent of education. He used several different forms and achieved successes in all of them, from the marvellous long lines of 'Remembrances' to the short couplets of 'Noon' and 'The fens'. He handled the complicated Spenserian stanza without effort and wrote some of his best poetry in that metre, and also left a particularly large number of superb sonnets (many of them constructed in an unconventional way). He wrote heroic couplets (in 'The parish') as good as Dryden's, produced parodies of other authors, and could turn out a competent imitation of Byron even when he was mad. Occasionally he used blank verse quite effectively; more often his poems rhyme, but (and this is one of the hardest tests for a poet) the rhymes grow naturally out of the subject matter and are not there for their own sake. He could do virtually anything he liked with the English language.

What he did, in all the poems which matter, was to make the reader *see*. One would have thought that he had very little material. He did not roam about Europe like Byron and Shelley, nor did he live in a picturesque part of England like the Lake Poets. Instead he grew up in a small closed community where the children had very few stimuli (snail-shells and marbles were their main toys) and might have been expected to turn out backward, and where the scenery seemed, to most people, unbelievably dreary:

> So moping flat and low our valleys lie
> So dull and muggy is our winter sky
> Drizzling from day to day dull threats of rain
> And when that falls still threating on again
> From one wet week so great an ocean flows
> That every village to an island grows
> And every road for even weeks to come
> Is stopt and none but horsemen go from home
> And one wet night leaves travels best in doubt
> And horseback travel asks if floods are out

Such are the lowland scenes that winter gives
And strangers wonder where our pleasure lives

('Winter in the fens')

But the fens, as the poem of that name illustrates, are swarming with life. Clare compensated for his restricted subject matter by looking more deeply and seeing much more clearly than the average person. He is 'the finest naturalist in all English poetry' (Robinson and Summerfield, Introduction to the *Shepherd's Calendar*), describing every species of bird, animal or insect life which came to his attention with unrivalled freshness and accuracy. He knew every tree for miles around Helpstone and regretted them bitterly when they were cut down. He also tells us a great deal, in his earlier poetry, about Helpstone people. All of them are distinct personalities; the cottager with his prejudices; the 'sticking' woman; the nasty little boy in the *Shepherd's Calendar* (November) trying to splash passers-by. We see them, boys included, going about their normal work; this landscape has little to attract the tourist but is always seen as a setting for human labour:

Muffled in baffles leathern coat and gloves
The hedger toils oft scaring rustling doves
From out the hedgrows who in hunger browze
The chockolate berrys on the ivy boughs
And flocking field fares speckld like the thrush
Picking the red awe from the sweeing bush
That come and go on winters chilling wing
And seem to share no sympathy wi spring
The stooping ditcher in the water stands
Letting the furrowd lakes from off the lands
Or splashing cleans the pasture brooks of mud
Where many a wild weed freshens into bud
And sprouting from the bottom purply green
The water cresses neath the wave is seen
Which the old woman gladly drags to land
Wi reaching long rake in her tottering hand
The ploughman mauls along the doughy sloughs

And often stop their songs to clean their ploughs
From teazing twitch that in the spongy soil
Clings round the colter terrifying toil
The sower striding oer his dirty way
Sinks anckle deep in pudgy sloughs and clay
And oer his heavy hopper stoutly leans
Strewing wi swinging arms the pattering beans

(*The Shepherd's Calendar*, 'March')

Perhaps it was a mistake to call the landscape a 'setting'. Labourers, birds and plants are all equally important here, and all equally dependent on the land for their existence. The work is heavy and dirty; the doves and the old woman are only just managing to stay alive. The agricultural year has its festivals, like the June sheep-shearing, but, on the whole, village life is hard. Labourers such as the woodman and 'the boy that pecks the turnips all the day/And knocks his hands to keep the cold away' ('Sheep in winter') have to go on working through heatwaves, mud and snow (and are not sorry when they can take a break during a shower). Sunday is particularly important to them, as their only free day:

A six days prisoner lifes support to earn
From dusty cobwebs and the murky barn
The weary thresher meets the rest thats given
And thankful sooths him in the boon of heaven

('Sunday walks')

Clare tells us that he usually spent his Sundays in the fields, in the company of shepherds, herdboys, and sometimes gipsies. It was a very positive experience; although he generally claimed to be a middle-of-the-road Christian he felt closer to God in the open air, 'far from terrors that the parson brings' ('Rustic fishing'), than in the parish church which was dominated by the village magnates anyway. The poor, he insisted, needed time and space to recover from their work, respond to nature and develop their individual interests. For him this meant, among other things, writing poetry; for others it might mean fishing, spending time with their children or cultivating flowers. He is always interested in their beliefs, their

210

behaviour when away from work, their relationship with their environment. This helps us to understand his fury at what was being done to the landscape.

Poems like the early 'Lamentations of Round-Oak Waters' and 'To a fallen elm', with the later and better 'The mores' (sometimes called 'Enclosure') and 'The lament of Swordy Well', passionately protest against the attitude that 'uneconomic' bits of land must, at all costs, make a profit. All of them, incidentally, remained unpublished until the twentieth century, and reveal a tough radical Clare of whom the Victorians would not have approved. In 'Round-Oak Waters' and 'Swordy Well', unusually, he gives the landscape a voice; the stream and the old stone quarry both protest against their treatment. He had often gone to Swordy Well to collect ferns and to admire the rare butterflies which lived there; now the place was being so ruthlessly exploited that neither people, nor plants, nor 'things that creep or flye' could derive any benefit from it:

> And me they turned me inside out
> For sand and grit and stones
> And turned my old green hills about
> And pickt my very bones.

'The mores' makes a near-identical point. Before enclosure, the poor could feed their animals on common land and enjoy a sense of space and freedom, flowers grew and birds were free to fly where they wished. Now they are cut up into 'little parcels little minds to please' – men are reduced, Clare suggests, by the lust to own property. In both poems, he accuses the people responsible of being 'philistines', 'vulgar', 'tasteless'; that is, of having no finer human sensibilities. The village politicians in 'The parish', 'churchwardens, constables and overseers', have 'learning just enough to sign a name/And skill sufficient parish rates to frame/And cunning deep enough the poor to cheat'. Clare believed that the 'educated' classes in Helpstone were, in fact, only half-literate and wholly lacking in the eighteenth-century virtue of 'taste'. (Robert Tressell made the same point about the Town Council or Forty Thieves of Mugsborough in *The Ragged-Trousered Philanthropists*.) It throws an interesting light on our own belief that he was a semi-educated 'peasant'.

For, of course, Clare was never a peasant but a landless labourer. Even his favourite elm trees behind the cottage where he lived did not belong to him but could be cut down when the landlord wanted to make a profit. 'To a fallen elm' comments:

> With axe at root he felled thee to the ground
> And barked of freedom – O I hate that sound
>
> It grows the cant terms of enslaving tools
> To wrong another by the name of right . . .
> Thus came enclosure – ruin was her guide
> But freedoms clapping hands enjoyed the sight
> Tho comforts cottage soon was thrust aside
> And workhouse prisons raised upon the scite
> Een natures dwelling far away from men
> The common heath became the spoilers prey
> The rabbit had not where to make his den
> And labours only cow was drove away
> No matter – wrong was right and right was wrong
> And freedoms brawl was sanction to the song

Here the word 'freedom' is used contemptuously; in other poems, like 'The mores', it has a positive value. It is a double-edged word for Clare; less important than the freedom to hold property is the freedom to satisfy basic human needs. One of these needs is the preservation of open spaces, in which all forms of life can flourish. Although the word 'ecologist' had not been invented in his time, Clare shared many of the insights of the modern 'green movement', a name which would have pleased him. Like them, he insisted that man does not own the earth and is not entitled to do whatever he likes with it. Instead he must treat it as a responsible steward, for his own sake and that of the other species (rabbits, elms, cattle) which also have a right to exist. He was so convinced of this that he persisted in saying it even after he had gone mad, writing in 'London versus Epping Forest': 'I could not bear to see the tearing plough/Root up and steal the Forest from the poor'.

If the word 'freedom' is ambiguous, the words 'the poor' or 'the poor man' are not. He signed himself 'A Poor Man' in a letter of

1829–30 in which he noted that 'the poor have many oppressors and no voice to be heard above them'. 'I own Im poor like many more/But then the poor mun live', says the speaker in 'Swordy Well'. Clare was always concerned that the poor should live, in the fullest sense of the word. He felt himself to be one of the Helpstone people, even if they did not much like his poetry, and had a deep instinctive distrust of the rich and of all politicians. We may observe that he did not believe the newspapers when they told him that the French were about to invade, nor did he trust the local farmers when they talked about 'freedom' at the time of the 1832 Reform Bill. 'The terms wig and tory are nothing more in my mind than the left and right hand of that monster.' (Note the crazy punning on the word 'wig' in 'Don Juan'.) Conversely, his sympathy always went out to those who had been ill-used – paupers, unmarried mothers, hunted birds and animals. The gipsies were particularly important in his scheme of things because they represented people living outside society and obeying only the laws of their own nature. They are anarchic but non-violent, living as the birds do by picking up what they can get. Clare does not sentimentalize them, but he does feel that they do less harm than many respectable citizens.

It had been different, he thought, in the past. There had once been a time 'when masters made them merry wi their men' (*The Shepherd's Calendar*, 'June'), farmers and labourers drinking furmety out of the same bowl. From what we know of the history of the Clare family, this may sound unlikely. But the idea of a vanished golden age fitted in with memories of a childhood before familiar trees had been cut down, fields enclosed and himself put out to work. Like Wordsworth, and, earlier, Henry Vaughan, he constantly writes about how happy he had been as a boy. It was a time when he could freely enjoy his beloved natural world. 'Each noise that breathed around us then/Was magic all and song', he wrote in 'Childhood', and, as an adult, nature still gave him the same sense of excitement.

THE FINEST NATURALIST IN ALL ENGLISH POETRY

To quote Johnson again, 'the business of a poet . . . is to examine, not the individual, but the species . . . he does not number the streaks of the tulip, or describe the different shades in the verdure of the forest'. Clare ignored this advice. He habitually counted the eggs in birds' nests and noted how 'the odd number five' kept appearing in nature – five spots in the cowslip and five streaks in the cup of the pink bindweed ('The eternity of nature'). In all his work, prose as well as poetry, he is concerned to describe what he has seen as accurately as possible:

> once when I was a young man on staying late at a feast I crossd a meadow about midnight and saw to my supprise quantitys of small nimble things emigrating across it a long way from any water   I thought at first they were snakes but I found on a closer observation that they were young eels making for a large pond calld the Islet pool which they journeyd to with as much knowledge as if they were acquainted with their way   I thought this a wonderful discovery then but I have since observd the same thing in larger eels going from one pond to another in the day time and I caught two very large ones in the act of emigrating

We find the same vivid and precise description in his earliest poems – beetles 'with jetty jackets glittering in the sun' ('Helpstone'); house martins' 'snowy breasts bedawbd in dirt' ('Summer evening'). On the whole he is less likely to write about flowers – although the 'Ragwort' sonnet is a splendid exception – than about the various kinds of wildlife around Helpstone. Just as we can trust his descriptions of seasonal activities in *The Shepherd's Calendar*, so we can believe in the reality of his birds eating haws and ivy berries; the mice running out of the corn when it is cut: the black bee 'that indian-like bepaints its little thighs/With white and red bedight for holiday' ('Wild bees'). This tendency to write in detail about everything he saw is so marked that some of his admirers, like Geoffrey Grigson, have felt it necessary to say that Clare was 'more than the poet of the *minutiae* of description' (Introduction to *Poems of John Clare's Madness*, 1949).

It is not, perhaps, a bad thing to have the gift of describing a creature or object in all its minute particulars. But there is a guiding principle behind Clare's nature poetry. His feeling, while he counts the streaks of the tulip, is of wonder at the life which pulses through each entity, an awareness of the dangers it faces, and an intense desire to write about it before it is lost. 'There was much about Clare for a Quaker to like; he was tender-hearted and averse to violence', wrote the poet Hood, who met him in London. In another of his nature letters he says:

> for my part I love to look on nature with a poetic feeling which magnifys the pleasure . . . I love to see the nightingale in its hazel retreat and the cuckoo hiding in its solitudes of oaken foliage and not to examine their carcasses in glass cages yet naturalists and botanists seem to have no taste for this poetical feeling . . . well every one to his hobby I have none of this curosity about me tho I feel as happy as they can in finding a new species of field flower or butter flye which I have not seen before yet I have no desire further to dry the plant or torture the Butterflye by sticking it on a cork board with a pin – I have no wish to do this if my feelings woud let me I only crop the blossom of the flower or take the root from its solitudes if it woud grace my garden and wish the fluttering butterflye to settle till I can come up with it to examine the powderd colours on its wings and then it may dance off from fancyd dangers and welcome.

Note that phrase 'I love' – 'I love to see' – which we find time and again in Clare's poetry. Sometimes, of course, it makes a good starting point for a piece of description (in the extract from 'Summer images' we can see how the words 'I love' are used to introduce a long series of things which the poet might expect to see on a summer morning). However, Clare really did love nature with a special passion. 'I lovd to see the heaving grasshopper in his coat of delicate green bounce from stub to stub' – he tells us of himself as a boy – 'I listend the hedgecricket with raptures.' Evidently it did not have to be particularly striking or beautiful. He notes, in 'The flitting', that an unpretentious little plant like the shepherd's purse has outlasted civilizations, and when in 1825 he found a quantity of snail-shells in the old Roman bank he remarked that the armies who built their straight roads through Northamptonshire 'little thought that the house of a poor simple snail horn woud outlive them'.

215

The species survives; the individual does not. Especially in his bird and animal poems, Clare is preoccupied with the fact, ignored by more sentimental writers, that nature is ruthless. In a lovely sonnet, 'Partridge coveys', he enumerates some of the threats faced by birds, incidentally registering the fact that life is hard for the gleaners too:

> Among the stubbles when the fields grow grey
> And mellow harvest gathers to a close
> The painful gleaner twenty times a day
> Start up the partridge broods that glad repose
> Upon the grassy slip or sunny land
> Yet ever it would seem in dangers way
> Where snufting dogs their rustling haunts betray
> And tracking gunners ever seem at hand
> Oft frighted up they startle to the shade
> Of neighbouring wood and through the yellow leaves
> Drop wearied where the brakes and ferns hath made
> A solitary covert – that decieves
> For there the fox prowls its unnoticed round
> And danger dares them upon every ground

Dogs, gunners, foxes, these are a few of the dangers, and elsewhere he mentions cats, snakes, oxen trampling along the footpath where lark and willow-warbler build their nests, and boys hunting for eggs. We generally believe that people who grow up in the countryside have little sympathy for birds and animals; Clare himself had certainly robbed nests as a boy. But, as he illustrates through the character of Lubin in 'The village minstrel', he had always been uncomfortably sensitive. In that poem, he tells us that traditional sports like badger-baiting and cock-fighting were too 'barbarous' for him, and as he grew older he felt more and more sympathy with hunted creatures. Many of his most impressive poems are about birds and their nests, which he describes in loving detail – 'deadend green or rather olive brown' ('The nightingale's nest'), 'pen-scribbled over lilac shells/Resembling writing scrawls' ('The yellowhammers nest'). An egg is certainly one of the lower forms of life, but, to Clare, all life is precious. In the marvellous 'Pettichaps nest', a much more sophisticated poem than it appears on first reading, he makes us

"When boys throw stones at frogs, they do so in sp
But when the frogs die, they die in earnest."

feel that the survival of the eggs, 'scarce bigger e'en then peas', against all the odds, is 'a miracle'. Again, in 'The groundlark', another poem about a bird who raises her brood under almost impossible conditions, his sense of relief at the end is unmistakable:

> The schoolboy kicked the grass in play
> But danger never guest
> And when they came to mow the hay
> They found an empty nest

Most of the time he is fairly objective about the realities of the struggle for existence. In the sonnet beginning 'The schoolboys in the morning soon as drest' he shows how, after the boys have rifled the chaffinch's nest, life goes on in the normal way:

> Heres eggs they hollowed with a hearty shout
> Small round and blotched they reached and tore them out
> The old birds sat and hollowed pink pink pink
> And cattle hurried to the pond to drink

The last line places what has gone before; cattle and schoolboys have their own preoccupations and anything the parent birds may be feeling does not count. But in other poems, particularly those written in the 1830s when his mind was beginning to give way, his personal outrage breaks in. In 'Remembrances' he wants to hide his face at the sight of the dead moles – 'O it turns my bosom chill'; the moles are victims of enclosure just as much as the Helpstone people. In another poem from the dark years, 'The hedgehog', the cruelty obviously sickens him:

> But still they hunt the hedges all about
> And shepherd dogs are trained to hunt them out
> They hurl with savage force the stick and stone
> And no one cares and still the strife goes on

but it is clear from that last, roughly written line that he knows his protest will lead nowhere. 'None shall break ranks', as Wilfred Owen was to write. By this time Clare was beginning to feel absolutely isolated; soon afterwards, he was in the asylum at Epping Forest.

We have pointed out that, in many of Clare's earlier poems, he was describing the work, pleasures and way of life of a whole community. In *The Shepherd's Calendar*, that marvellous account of an English village from January to December, which really needs to be read as a whole, there is no sense of separation between the poet and the people he is writing about. He sympathizes and identifies with them, having sprung from their ranks himself; even when he points out (as in 'The cottager') that they have various prejudices and limitations, his satire is gentle. However, it was a community that treated him with suspicion. His autobiography and 'The fate of genius' show that he had to put up with a certain amount of spite because he presumed to be different from his neighbours, as does a savage little verse:

> Goosey goosey gander
> Where would you wander
> Up the fen and down the fen
> To cackle and to slander.

Even in the very early 'Helpstone', we can see that he felt he was searching in vain for a 'better life', and that his beloved village was the home of 'useless ignorance'. So his feelings were highly ambiguous. He became extremely depressed when he moved away from his birthplace, yet he needed to leave it occasionally, to meet other poets and to make contact with educated people. Having left his own class, it was not possible for him to join another; the people who had bought his first book of poems because it was by a Northamptonshire peasant ignored his later and much better work. During the 1820s and 1830s his reputation waned, money troubles accumulated and, although Patty should not be blamed, he probably felt that he had made the wrong marriage. With Blake he might have written 'O why was I born with a different face?/Why was I not born like this envious race?' This is probably what every sensitive person has felt at times, and Clare had long known that he was much too sensitive. (But could he have written poetry like that, if it had not been so?) Writing about his distress when the elms were cut down, he acknowledged, 'I am a fool were people all to feel as I do the world coud not be carried on'.

There is a certain kind of protest poetry which is directed only against specific evils. 'The parish' and some of the anti-enclosure poems, for all their vigour, belong to this group. Here, he appears to be saying that life used to be good and might be good again if the village magnates behaved better, or if enclosure was stopped. But during his last years of freedom, Clare was moving towards a more basic kind of protest. It was an outcry against what most people consider the normal conditions of life, and this can very easily spill over into madness. His private problems, man's cruelty to animals, the condition of England, all seemed to him aspects of the central evil:

> This life is made of lying and grimace
> This world is filled with whoring and deceiving
> Hypocrisy ne'er masks an honest face
> Story's are told – but seeing his believing
> And I've seen much from which there's no retrieving
> I've seen deception take the place of truth
> I've seen knaves flourish – and the country grieving
> Lies was the current gospel in my youth
> And now a man – I'm farther off from truth

In the same poem, 'Child Harold', composed after his breakdown, he wrote, 'I envy birds their wings to fly away'. He had always been fascinated by creatures which avoided human haunts – the 'oddling' crow, the 'hermit' sand martin, the snipe. Now, as far as possible, he turned his back on his own kind:

> My themes be artless cots and happy plains
> Though far from man my wayward fancies flee
> Of fields and woods rehearse in willing strains

('Child Harold')

He retained his need for love, hence the poems to Mary and to various other women of whom we know nothing but their names. But the nature poetry written during the asylum years describes a landscape empty of people, in which only birds and growing things are significant. The two long pieces, 'Don Juan' and 'Child Harold', are a crazy jumble of love ditties, diatribes against politicians, desperate appeals to God, references to his 'two wives'. But one theme which constantly recurs – it inspires several beautiful passages in 'Child Harold' – is that nature is a healing force. The sea (which he had seen only once, at Boston) became a symbol of everything that frightened him; the solid earth and sky meant repose and stability:

> I see the sky
> Smile on the meanest spot
> Giving to all that creep or walk or flye
> A calm and cordial lot

he had written long before, in 'The snipe'. In 'I am', the most famous of his mad poems, the 'vaulted sky' and 'grass below' seem to offer some kind of refuge from the turmoil within his mind. By the time he had been confined for a few years he was capable only of writing fairly short poems, often simple lyrics like this one:

> Look through the naked bramble and black thorn
> And see the arum show its vivid green
> Glossy and rich and some ink spotted like the morn
> Ing sky with clouds – in sweetest neuks Ive been
> And seen the arum sprout its happy green

In this little poem, the word 'green' is constantly repeated, as it is in the better-known 'Solitude'. The world, with its manifold evils, cannot satisfy basic human needs; the person who has been 'wounded' by it does well to shun everything except nature – a claim made by Hardy half a century later, in 'Wessex Heights'.

> There is a charm in Solitude that cheers
> A feeling that the world knows nothing of
> A green delight the wounded mind endears
> After the hustling world is broken off
> Whose whole delight was crime at good to scoff
> Green solitude his prison pleasure yields
> The bitch fox heeds him not – birds seem to laugh
> He lives the Crusoe of his lonely fields
> Which dark green oaks his noontide leisure shields

Clare was mad; no one who met him in his later years was in any doubt about that. But he continued to write poetry which speaks to our condition in a way that more 'normal' and rational writers often fail to do. We admire him not only because he had a marvellous command of language but also because we instinctively sympathize with his feelings about the world he found himself in. Clare understood, as we are beginning to understand, that no one can really be a Crusoe; all human beings need a satisfying relationship with society and with the natural world if they are to retain their psychic health. After 200 years, how contemporary he seems!

Further reading

The Oxford Authors: John Clare (Oxford, 1984), edited by Eric Robinson and David Powell. Presents most of Clare's best poems and some of the prose in the most authentic form available.

The Shepherd's Calendar (Oxford, 1964), edited by Eric Robinson and Geoffrey Summerfield, and *The Parish* (London, 1985), edited by Eric Robinson. The most reliable texts for Clare's two longest poems.

The Poems of John Clare (London, 1935), edited by J. W. Tibble. Textually unreliable, but contains some good poems not found elsewhere.

Poems of John Clare's Madness (London, 1949), edited by Geoffrey Grigson. Should be read for the Introduction.

Selected Poems and Prose of John Clare (Oxford, 1967), edited by Eric Robinson and Geoffrey Summerfield.

Sketches in the Life of John Clare (London, 1931), edited by Edmund Blunden. A short account of Clare's early life by himself.

The Prose of John Clare (London, 1951), edited by J. W. and Anne Tibble. Includes a fragmentary autobiography, journal and nature notes.

The Life of John Clare (London, 1865), by Frederick W. Martin. Vivid, fascinating but not always accurate biography, best read in the second edition (London, 1964) with an introduction and notes by Eric Robinson and Geoffrey Summerfield.

John Clare: A Life (London, 1972) by J. W. and Anne Tibble. The fullest modern biography.

Useful critical works are: *Clare: The Critical Heritage* (London, 1973), ed. Mark Storey; *The Idea of Landscape and the Sense of Place 1730–1840: An Approach to the Poetry of John Clare* (Cambridge, 1972), by John Barrell; *The Poetry of John Clare, A Critical Introduction* (London, 1974), by Mark Storey; *John Clare and the Folk Tradition* (London, 1983), by George Deacon; and *John Clare and Picturesque Landscape* (Oxford, 1983), by Timothy Brownlow. A more general discussion of forms of country writing, including an analysis of Clare, is in *The Country and the City* (London, 1973), by Raymond Williams.

Notes

HELPSTONE

This poem, written when Clare was very young, shows the influence of Goldsmith's 'Deserted Village' (1770). 'I hinted to you that I had seen the Deserted Village', he wrote, 'you may think I imitated it I saw it as I have seen a many dipping into it here and there I perhaps may have read a hundred lines . . . I am not a plagarist I beg you to compare them together and then the difference will be seen.'

Both poems are written in the same style – heroic couplets – and each poet laments a happy past, writing about affection for an old village and sorrow at the destruction of landmarks. Goldsmith denounces a society 'where wealth accumulates, and men decay'; Clare too is angry at 'accursed wealth' that 'levels every tree' (ll. 127 and 133) and at the treatment of the labourers. But while 'The Deserted Village' is quite unambiguous, 'Helpstone' is not. The first two sections make it obvious that Clare was not completely happy in Helpstone and had had dreams of a 'better life' (l. 25).

Clare's patron, Lord Radstock, objected to the passage beginning, 'Accursed wealth o'er bounding human laws' (ll. 127–34) because of its 'radical and ungrateful sentiments', and it was left out of the fourth edition, much against Clare's will.

7–12   *Where dawning genius . . . humble view*   Clare is referring to his early struggles to get his poetry published and his neighbours' hostility.

53	*those years of infancy* the first of many references to his happy childhood.
73–5	*The vanish'd green . . . the brook is gone* He is referring to the effects of enclosure.
89	*e'en a post* It will be seen that Clare disliked even the smallest changes in his environment.
106	*shepherd's woolly charge* i.e. sheep. The young Clare often used this kind of 'poetic' language.
116	*The pride of life with thee (like mine) is oer* Clare could hardly have been more than 20 when he wrote this.
177–8	*all my troubles past . . . die at home at last* a direct borrowing from Goldsmith's poem, which runs

> I still had hopes, my long vexations past,
> Here to return – and die at home at last.

NOON

18	The quotation is from 'Day', by John Cunningham (1729–73), and Clare wished to alter it.
21	*love's oaten strains* He is referring to the oat stems traditionally used as a musical pipe by shepherds.
53	*O poor birds* one of the earliest references to Clare's sympathy for wildlife.

THE HARVEST MORNING

35	*horns* Bits of barley have got into his clothes.
39–46	Clare goes straight from description to moral commentary, and these lines show his sympathy with the poor.
59	*the beavering hour* the labourers' meal break.

THE LAMENTATIONS OF ROUND-OAK WATERS

Round Oak Waters is the stream issuing from Round Oak spring in Royce Wood. When Clare wrote this the trees and meadows by this stream had disappeared and the labourers' lives had grown harder, deprived as they were of green spaces to rest in.

1	*double share* The poet is grieved by his own problems, but also by what has been done to the landscape.
65	*Cowboy* Clare often refers to 'cowboys' – who are simply boys who mind cows.
72–92	Note that even as a boy Clare was the odd one out.
101–12	*bawks* and *Eddings* are words to be noticed. These strips of green land which separated the ploughed fields (rather than hedges) had a great emotional significance for Clare.
141	*T—1* Richard Turnill, a friend who died young.
182–6	It is not obvious why some words are represented by dashes; perhaps Clare felt that certain sentiments were too explosive to print. The radical tone of the last four verses is very pronounced.

from SUMMER EVENING

This poem begins as a straight description of a summer evening, but turns into a diatribe against cruelty.

53–5	The driver and ox (*ball*) are bringing home the heavy roller used for breaking clods. *Doll* is a generic name for milk-maids.
95	*kill em O in cruel pride* The 'O' in mid sentence shows Clare's uncontrollable distress on behalf of the sparrows. Boys were paid to kill them.

MY MARY

This is written in the same style, and with the same refrain, as a sad and rather lovely poem by Cowper. It was omitted from later editions of Clare's first book because some readers were offended by its racy language. 'Mary' is unlikely to be Mary Joyce, for whom he had much more 'poetic' feelings.

SUMMER

This is one of the earliest of Clare's many superb sonnets and shows how skilfully he could handle the form. Most of them are not strictly

'Petrarchan' or 'Shakespearean' but follow a pattern of his own choosing.

LANGLEY BUSH

Langley Bush was an old whitethorn that according to Clare had 'stood for more then a century . . . Gipseys Shepherds and Herdmen all had their tales of its history'. It finally fell in 1823.

THE WOODMAN

This is one of Clare's best and most ambitious early poems, though not faultless.

19–23   Note the realism of the details – porridge and barley crust – followed by the not very realistic 'as happily as princes and as kings'.

46ff   The close observation, in this verse, of animals in winter, can be compared with that in *The Shepherd's Calendar*, 'November'.

59   *lawrence wages*   St Lawrence is the patron of idleness. The line can be translated 'when the weather invites people to be lazy'.

71–2   *'serning* – discerning – and *'clement* – inclement – are abbreviations put in only to make the lines scan, and they sound awkward. See also *'crease* in l. 102.

115   *Self heal* and *agrimony* are both fairly common wild flowers. Self heal was traditionally used for cuts and sore throats; agrimony for liver complaints.

165   *loves last pledge*   the youngest child.

202   *burred moons*   a ring round the moon.

217   *Holland*   Isaiah Knowles Holland was the Congregational minister at Market Deeping, and Clare's friend. The last verse sounds mechanical, and could well have been left out.

In this poem Clare describes in detail his belief – like Wordsworth's in the 'Immortality Ode' – that his childhood was his happiest time and that since then (see ll. 35–6) his feelings have been blunted.

9   His fondness for *trifling things* is very characteristic. Note the importance he gives to the shepherd's purse in 'The flitting'.

30   *pootey shell* Clare refers several times to snail-shells, which were obviously a significant part of his childhood games.

THE GIPSEYS CAMP

Clare tells us that he often went to the gipsies' camps on Sundays or summer evenings and was tempted to join them. This poem shows that he did not romanticize them – 'they are deceitful generally and have a strong propensity to lying yet they are not such dangerous characters as some in civilized life'.

'MY FIRST ATTEMPTS AT POETRY'

19ff   See 'A Sunday with shepherds and herdboys'.

from THE VILLAGE MINSTREL

This is an extract from a much longer poem. The child 'Lubin' (l. 234), born sensitive and a nonconformist, is Clare.

225   *His numbers* his poems.
257–70 *Old senseless gossips . . . morning, noon, and night* Obviously Clare found village life limited and limiting from a very early age.
271–9 *Nor sabbath-days . . . pain* Clare comments elsewhere, notably in 'The parish', on the religious indifference of congregations.

Another lament for the chopping down of trees in Helpstone. The fourth verse again links the poet's childhood to a happy time before enclosure.

NOON

13   This line should be read 'O for a sudden shower free from thunder'.

from RURAL EVENING

This extract shows Clare's talent for detailed description, and his interest in how labourers spend their free time.

111   *share* ploughshare.

'GOING FOR A SOLDIER'

20   *the rebellion of '45* the Jacobite rising of 1745.
31   *going to Botany Bay* being transported.

from THE FATE OF GENIUS

The 'rustic genius' of this poem is of course Clare himself, seen through the eyes of a puzzled acquaintance. It owes something to the end of Gray's 'Elegy written in a country churchyard', and gives a pathetic picture of the poet dying from the effects of spiteful treatment by his neighbours.

61–2   *tyrant boys ... sparrows* See the note on 'Summer evening'.
80   Evidently Clare's contemporaries believed in ghosts, though he did not.

A PROPHET IS NOTHING IN HIS OWN COUNTRY

2   *Drury* Edward Drury, the Stamford bookseller who helped the poet to publish his early work.

Lolham Bridge, near Castor, carries the old Roman road, Ermine Street, over the Welland. According to his publisher, Clare was there on the last day of March, 1821, and 'the triumph of true genius seemed never more conspicuous, than in the construction of so interesting a poem out of such commonplace materials. With your own eyes you see nothing but a dull line of ponds, or rather one continued marsh, over which a succession of arches carries the narrow highway. . . . Imagination has, in my opinion, done wonders here.'

67–8   *The moor hen . . . destroying boys* Note Clare's preoccupation with birds' nests and eggs, and the threats to them from boys and others.

97   *the work of Roman hands* There were several traces of the Romans around Helpstone. Clare was very conscious of the fact that civilizations decay while nature remains much the same.

TO A FALLEN ELM

Clare apparently wrote this poem when the landlord was threatening to cut down the elm behind his parents' cottage, which was intertwined with his earliest memories. 'The savage who owns them thinks they have done their best and now he wants to make use of the benefits he can get from selling them.' The four long sections are all sonnets of various sorts.

42   *Bawl freedom loud* For his attitude to freedom, see the Critical commentary, p. 212.

69   *knaves that brawl for better laws* Landowners who want votes but ruthlessly exploit the class below them, and the environment.

from A SUNDAY WITH SHEPHERDS AND HERDBOYS

Like the gipsies, though not so obviously, Clare's shepherds and herdboys are outside respectable society and have their own customs and ethics.

33   *checkering*   The villages make a pattern on the landscape resembling a chessboard.

37   *lapt up to lare*   The leafy 'grots' are hiding-places for animals.

55   *near*   never. Clare suggests here as elsewhere that although the farmers go to church regularly their real concern is money.

63–4   *pilferd wood . . . stolen food*   The shepherds have little respect for property, but this does not seem to upset Clare.

88   *That live like flowers in rural vales*   This is a beautiful image for the survival of traditional tales in small closed communities with little printed literature.

THE MORES

This is Clare's own title; some editors call the poem 'Enclosure'. It is an impassioned attack on those who have caused the moors to suffer the fate of the commons, turning men and animals off the land in pursuit of gain. The phrase *little tyrant* (l. 67) is borrowed from Gray's 'Elegy', but he uses the word 'little' very effectively as a term of contempt: *In little parcels little minds to please* (l. 49); the essence of the moors is that they seem boundless.

7   *Unbounded freedom ruled the wandering scene*   Below, we find that the sheep and cows feel 'free' on the moors (ll. 23 and 28), as do the lark and plover (ll. 34 and 38), but by the end 'men and flocks' are 'imprisoned' (l. 50), and 'with the poor scared freedom bade good bye' (l. 75). Freedom is the central concept in this poem.

27   *unfolded*   released from the fold.

46   *Like mighty giants of their limbs bereft*   This is a very powerful image; the moors are still there but have lost their most characteristic quality.

54   *travel*   the traveller.

65   The enclosers are philistines because they have no eyes for natural beauty. See also 'vulgar taste' in l. 72.

69   *to freedom and to childhood dear*   As in many of Clare's

poems, freedom and childhood are practically the same
thing.

THE LAMENT OF SWORDY WELL

Like 'The mores', this poem is directed against the exploitation of
the land for gain. Swordy or Swaddy Well was an ancient stone
quarry where Clare used to go to collect ferns and observe butterflies. He wrote that the pasque flower (now rare) 'grows on the
roman bank agen Swordy well and did grow in great plenty but the
plough that destroyer of wild flowers has rooted it out'.

45	*grubbling geer*	The grub-axe was used to uproot plants.
49	*When war their tyrant prices got*	The Napoleonic Wars had pushed up the price of corn.
73ff.	The animals which can no longer get a living from the land are compared to the poor who are being forced into the workhouse.	
166	*God send the grain to fall*	If grain were cheap, the land might be less ruthlessly exploited.
169	*I was kind to all*	Compare with the lines:

> Thoust sheltered hypocrites in many a shower
> That when in power would never shelter thee
> ('To a fallen elm')

179	*The ass no pindard dare to pound*	The pound was a pen for stray animals; the pindar the man responsible for putting them there.
181	Note the importance of gipsies as a symbol of freedom.	

from THE PARISH

These are extracts from a long poem (over 2000 lines) which, Clare
wrote, was

> begun and finished under the pressure of heavy distress with
> embittered feelings under a state of anxiety and oppression almost
> amounting to slavery – when the prosperity of one class was

founded on the adversity and distress of the other – The haughty demand by the master to his labourer was work for the little I chuse to allow you and go to the parish for the rest – or starve – to decline working under such advantages was next to offending a magistrate and no oppertunity was lost in marking the insult by some unquallified oppression.

He worked on it over a period of years and said in 1826 that it was 'the best thing in my own mind that I have ever written'.

He mentions 'that good old fame the farmers earnd of yore/That made as equals not as slaves the poor', and he praises the late vicar, but he believed that the poor in his own time were treated brutally by the village ruling class. The poem, never published in his lifetime, is a most effective satire in the style and tradition of Dryden and Pope.

The quotation is from Pope's 'Advertisement' to his 'Epistle to Dr Arbuthnot'.

'Village patriots'

Brag is of course not a real person but a type of the men who in the years before the Reform Bill of 1832 espoused 'patriotic' or progressive views which seemed phoney to Clare because they were not concerned with the needs of his own class.

746   *Fool in his own [affairs] but wonderous wise in theirs*   He thinks himself an expert on politics but cannot do his own job and has no compassion for the poor.
770   William Cobbett (1763–1835), the author of *Rural Rides* and a leading radical journalist.
790   *the good old cause*   parliamentary reform.
794   *dirty flags*   Clare constantly uses images of dirt in this poem to convey his contempt for people like Brag. Note also the 'dung hill' in line 804.

'The parish council'

1220   *Overseers*   officials responsible for poor relief.
1229   *darkness visible*   The phrase is borrowed from Milton's

Paradise Lost, but here the line means that they cannot help showing their own stupidity.

1264   *Sancho*   like Sancho Panza in Cervantes' *Don Quixote*, a servant.

1276–7   *Hudibrass ... Ralph* The reference is to *Hudibras* (published 1662–80), by Samuel Butler. Sir Hudibras and his squire Ralph are comic characters who cause endless trouble.

1310   *Tyburn tree*   the gallows.

1324ff   The poor who stole because they were desperate were liable to be hanged for it.

1355   *Want*   Clare uses the collective noun, as in 'labour'.

'The workhouse'

In this powerful passage Clare argues that the paupers are not even allowed sunlight or a patch of garden. His theme – the sheer meanness of the system – is very like that of 'Swordy Well', and his feelings about the workhouse were shared by most of the rural poor. His own parents narrowly escaped going there in 1819.

TO THE SNIPE

One of the longest and most impressive of Clare's bird poems. The snipe, like the poet, is a lover of solitude, and he feels an affinity with it. He had seen them at Whittlesey Mere, drained in 1850.

39   *Hiding in spots that never knew his tread*   See 'I long for scenes where man hath never trod' in 'I am'.

THE WOODMAN

One of Clare's best early sonnets. The last two lines are very fine; Clare is evidently glad that the birds and flowers are not to be interfered with.

This is an affectionate piece of satire. Clare, too, had not often gone 50 miles from home (l. 6), but was obviously a great deal more sophisticated than the old man.

11	*steams almighty tales*	stories of steam engines.
19	*St Thomas tide*	St Thomas's Day is 21 December.
37	*chevey chase*	'Chevy Chase', a famous medieval ballad.
63	*Death of Abel*	(1761) by Salomon Gessner.

65   Thomas Tusser (*c.* 1524–80) was the author of *A Hundreth Good Points of Husbandrie* (1557), a very popular and often reprinted set of rhyming instructions on farming, gardening and housekeeping. Clare enjoyed reading it too.

81–2   Admiral Rodney defeated the French fleet under de Grasse in 1782 off Dominica. The Marquis of Granby's son was fatally wounded in the battle.

from THE SHEPHERD'S CALENDAR

This sequence of twelve poems about the progress of the year in an English village is one of Clare's finest works, although it was not appreciated in his own time. He used different metres for the different months.

from *June*

84   *pint horn*   The horn was an old-fashioned drinking vessel, and was being replaced by glasses. For Clare it seems to have symbolized traditional virtues. In the same way, the old beech bowl, from which all were welcome to drink, is an image of good fellowship, and when it is 'thrown aside' (l. 101), this is a bad omen.

88   *the good old times*   As in 'The parish', Clare laments the friendly relationship between farmers and men which seems to have gone for ever. See l. 101ff.

131   *Bess in her bravery*   This might be the double daisy.

November

This is the best of the twelve poems in *The Shepherd's Calendar*. With its weird atmosphere (owls coming out in daylight) and unusual imagery (billy goats and braying asses) it creates a memorable picture of land workers and animals coping with the bleak weather.

46 Bird-scaring boys used to be a common sight and are frequently found in literature – e.g. 'boys who in lone wheat-fields scare the rooks' in Arnold's 'Scholar gypsy', or Hardy's *Jude the Obscure*.

56 The *scarlet hunter* is a very small spot of brightness in the generally cold, dim atmosphere of this poem. Clare is more interested in the daily routine of the countryside than in those who are merely passing through.

58 *sullen labour hath its tethering tye* The boy's life is unglamorous compared with the huntsman's.

69 *fallow stain* a pale brown colour.

90 *prophecys a storm* In chapter 36 of Hardy's *Far from the Madding Crowd*, country-dwellers are able to forecast a storm from the animals' behaviour.

154–61 This stanza is incomplete.

from CHILDHOOD

Again Clare remembers childhood happiness in the vein of Wordsworth, giving the impression that he is now fairly old and tired.

211 *Bounaparte* Napoleon, a bogeyman to English children.

255–6 See Wordsworth's 'Immortality Ode': 'To me the meanest flower that blows can give/Thoughts that do often lie too deep for tears.'

287–8 Oak apples were worn on 29 May within living memory to celebrate Charles II's escape from the Roundheads, after hiding in an oak tree.

'MEMORIES OF CHILDHOOD'

1 Clare described the joys of angling in a fine poem, 'Rustic fishing'.

68   Eastwell Spring is mentioned in 'Remembrances'.

71   Frumity or furmety, a popular old-fashioned drink made from grains of wheat boiled in milk. Hardy describes it in the first chapter of *The Mayor of Casterbridge*.

from SUMMER IMAGES

99   *I love* Note this key phrase of Clare's, which introduces a series of pictures. They are all quiet and unspectacular – the snail, which is described with great insight and sympathy, the frog and crickets, normal changes in light and weather.

149   *watchet* light-blue: an archaic word often used by Chatterton.

THE FLOOD

The three stanzas of this poem were printed separately for many years; it gains enormously when read as a whole. Written from the viewpoint of someone standing on Lolham Bridge (see 'The last of March') it shows the violence and destructive energies of nature.

EMMONSAILS HEATH IN WINTER

One of Clare's best-known sonnets, and one in which he appears to identify with other lonely beings, like herons and gipsies.

10   *thorn* There is no rhyme for this word; like many other sonnets of Clare's this one has no orthodox pattern.

ENGLAND, 1830

1830 was the year when agitation for parliamentary reform was at its height and when farm labourers were rioting in the south of England. As the last line suggests, Clare was sceptical about the value of any likely legislation.

SAND MARTIN

Another poem about a solitary bird (whose strange habits are described with great exactness) which rouses 'a feeling that I cant describe' in Clare.

THE THRUSHES NEST

13   *natures minstrels*   Even in a poem as good as this Clare does occasionally fall back on conventional phrases.

THE PETTICHAPS NEST

'A little bird about the size of a wren that has a note something like "Pettichap", whence its name', Clare wrote, and he gives it this name rather than the more poetical 'willow-warbler'. Note the skill with which he handles the rhyme-scheme in this and the next poem.

THE YELLOWHAMMERS NEST

18–19   *Castaly . . . parnass hill*   He compares the brook where the 'writing' bird lives to Castalia on Mount Parnassus, the fountain of the Muses.

'SNAKES'

5   *furze kidders*   workers who gather bundles of furze.
37   *oaking time*   peeling the bark of oaks to be used in tanning.

HEDGE SPARROW

As in most of Clare's poems about birds' eggs, the emphasis is on the dangers to their survival.

from THE FLITTING

Clare moved from Helpstone to Northborough in May 1832, and this poem, which begins 'I've left my own old home of homes', describes his depression. It was a very short move but had a devastating effect on him, 'Here every tree is strange to me'. He is consoled because, after all, he is still in touch with nature, and feels that 'passions of sublimity/Belong to plain and simpler things', such as the shepherd's purse which grew in his old garden. It is characteristic of him to be so moved by a common and ordinary-looking weed.

REMEMBRANCES

This poem, Clare's greatest elegy for the Helpstone of his childhood, has a startling power. It is hard to think of any other poem in this metre (a very difficult one to handle) which is anything like as good. The names all belong to trees or places around Helpstone.

5   *Dear heart*   The colloquial tone, as in 'The pettichaps nest', actually adds to the effect.

6   *Langley bush*   See the poem of that name.

8   These are all children's games played with marbles or pebbles.

11   *eastwells boiling spring*   Before enclosure people used to go to Eastwell Spring on Sundays and drink sugar and water.

15   *lea close oak*   a tree cut down in the enclosure programme.

24   *swordy well*   See 'The lament of Swordy Well'.

38   Significantly, the only tree that has not been cut down is used for hanging the moles.

51   *I never thought that joys would run away from boys*   The poem could easily turn into doggerel, but doesn't.

67   *Inclosure like a Buonaparte*   a striking image of self-interest run wild.

70   See 'The lamentations of Round-Oak Waters'.

THE FENS

This poem appears to be an ordinary pleasant piece of description at first, but Clare's preoccupation with the destruction of trees and meadows appears towards the end, 'Gain mars the landscape every day' (l. 84). The snake which we first hear of in l. 8 reappears in the last section, where references to toads, thistles, eating and killing give the poem sinister and depressing overtones. The fens are less innocent than they may seem.

THE PUDDOCK'S NEST

A puddock is a kite. This is one of Clare's darkest poems; the boys here are not content with taking eggs but <u>torture</u> the baby birds as well. The last couplet makes its protest <u>through</u> straightforward description. *Perhaps torture is too strong a word.*

11   *old ones*   presumably Clare meant to write 'young'.
                                          Not necessarily.

THE MARTEN

This poem seems not to have been quite finished; 'long shagged' is used twice in the first three lines and l. 5 does not scan. It was written at a time of increasing depression. The group of animal poems to which it belongs all show Clare's sympathy with hunted creatures, and his obsession with the struggle for existence in the wild, which both repelled and fascinated him.

7   *hides in lonely shade*   The cat is yet another hermit.
28   *free from boys and dogs and noise and men*   the condition to which Clare aspires.

THE FOX

28   *He lived to chase the hounds another day*   Clare is obviously not sorry; he admired qualities like the marten's 'courage good' and the fox's resourcefulness.

THE BADGER

Like 'The flood', this is a dynamic poem, full of violent activity. The atmosphere of savage struggle is conveyed with great power. In some versions it ends at l. 54, which is certainly a more dramatic climax.

THE HEDGEHOG

5   There are several time-honoured legends that hedgehogs
     pick up apples on their spines, milk the cows, etc. Clare
     has some sympathy with the gipsies who use them for
     food, but the practice of killing them because of these
     superstitions obviously revolts and disturbs him. The
     reward for a dead hedgehog was fourpence.

THE WATER LILIES

This poem, and the next two, were written during Clare's time at
High Beach Asylum. Their calmness contrasts with the obviously
unbalanced note of 'Don Juan'.

'BYRON'S FUNERAL'

Byron was buried on 14 July 1824.

DON JUAN A POEM

Clare re-read 'Don Juan' soon after Byron's death and wished 'that
the great poet had livd to finish it'. His own poem was written in
High Beach Asylum, after he had been reading it again, and is in the
same style; in certain moods, he believed that Byron was himself. As
the Tibbles say in their biography, it is 'an errant poem full of coarse-
ness straight out of a sub-conscious released from strain'. It is
dominated by a bitterness towards women (as in Shakespeare's
darker plays) for which there is no obvious reason. Other feelings
which come over strongly are Clare's dislike and distrust of
politicians and his belief that he had two wives, but the reader should
not expect it to make perfect sense.

38   *Commons* for cattle and *warrens* for rabbits – his old pre-
      occupations briefly re-emerge in this line.
48   Opposition to the corn laws which kept the price of bread
      high was very strong at this time.
63   *crim con*   criminal conversation, i.e. adultery.

72	Vulcan was married to Venus.
75–6	*wigs . . . beaten hollow* The Whigs had lost the election of July 1841.
80	To oil someone's wig – to make them drunk.
84	The papers had announced the marriage of Lord John Russell to Lady Fanny Elliott in July 1841.
103	Clare suggests that as soon as Albert is in Germany someone else will get the Queen with child.
113	Lord Melbourne ceased to be Prime Minister in August 1841. *little Vicky* – the Queen.
115	*the young princess* Queen Victoria's first child. A dickey was the driver's seat in a carriage.
116	*ass milk diet* often given to babies.
121	*These batch of toadstools on this rotten tree* This image very vividly suggests Clare's belief that society is wholly corrupt, and can produce nothing good.
152	*Eliza Phillips* not identified.
153–82	The 'Song' shows an abrupt change of mood; in it Clare dreams of love, freedom and nature. The 'forest' is Epping Forest where the asylum stood.
197	*Mary and Martha* Mary Joyce and his wife Patty, whose real name was Martha. He was very aware of the biblical significance of these names; Martha was the ordinary working wife, Mary the ideal.
223	*Docter Bottle* In 'The parish' Clare satirized a quack whom he called Doctor Urine.
227	*A–ll–n* Dr Matthew Allen, the superintendent of the asylum, and an enlightened man.
241	*fair young chicken* the Queen.
247	*Give toil more pay* Clare's inability to get a reasonable income probably contributed to his madness.
262	*Next tuesday* 13 July was Clare's birthday but not Byron's. In the next verse he claims that Byron is 'still in Allens madhouse caged and living'; in other moods he believed himself to be Queen Victoria's father.
276	*the 'Isle of Palms'* (1812), by 'Christopher North' (John Wilson).

Clare wrote a letter to Mary after he had got home saying that this account of his journey was 'for your amusement', although he was dimly aware that she was dead.

51   *the next village*   Baldock.

72   *makeing lace*   At the time lace-making was a very important cottage industry in Bedfordshire.

144   *St Ives*   in fact St Neot's.

224   *the old story of her being dead*   Mary Joyce had died in July 1838 and been buried in Glinton churchyard.

230–1   The quotation (slightly garbled) is from Byron's 'Sonnet on Chillon'.

from CHILD HAROLD

These are extracts from a very long poem (1300 lines), written in several different styles and uneven in quality. Clare began it at High Beach and continued working on it at home after his escape. The title is borrowed from Byron's 'Childe Harold's pilgrimage'. 'Childe' is a medieval term for a youth of noble birth. The passages in Spenserian stanzas make up a great poem of love and longing.

145   *My life hath been one love – no blot it out*   Clare feels that his life has been 'one chain of contradictions', perhaps because, in fantasy if not fact, he had 'two wives'. 'Real poets must be truly honest men', he said in line 3, but perhaps he felt this could not be said of him.

172   *this hill of fern*   He is describing the scenery at Epping Forest.

187   *Babes of two mothers*   Like the 'two wives', this was a delusion.

426   *Fame blazed upon me*   He is referring to the success of his first book of poems.

696–749 This section was written after Clare's escape, and makes it clear that he was happy to be at home again. The poetry is beautiful and soothing; as always, nature helped him to accept his difficulties. The reference to 'arches' in l. 719 is probably to Lolham Bridge.

TIS MARTINMAS FROM RIG TO RIG

This was also written during Clare's brief spell of freedom. St Martin's Day is 11 November.

LORD HEAR MY PRAYER WHEN TROUBLE GLOOMS

A paraphrase of the first seventeen verses of Psalm 102, and a very good one.

MARY

Clare knows that Mary is dead – 'Spirit of her I love' – yet he also believes that she is with him – 'the path on which *we* pass'. One reason why the poem is so affecting is because of his awareness of the gulf between what he wants and his actual situation.

SONG

5   *My life is like the ocean wave*   In this poem, like 'Song last day' and 'I am', Clare obviously feels that the sea represents a threat.

SONG LAST DAY

This and all the remaining poems were written at Northampton Asylum.

7   Clare uses the sea as a symbol of madness and alienation.

I AM

The poem by which Clare is best known, this perfectly expresses common feelings of alienation and a wish to return to a state of innocence. His first biographer, Frederick Martin, claimed that it was his last poem, but this is untrue.

11–12   thought to be a reference to the fact that his family seldom came to see him.

THE PEASANT POET

Clare had often been described under this name.

THE WINTERS COME

27   *old Bartons 'melancholy'* Robert Burton's *Anatomy of Melancholy*.

TO JOHN CLARE

Clare wrote this poem in February 1860 after a long silence. John Godfrey, secretary of the asylum, commented, 'The refreshing sweetness of these simple productions of the old poet's pen was very surprising to those who had noticed his desponding condition.'

12   *new number* a 'sixpenny romance', sold at the cottage doors by hawkers.

LETTER TO JAMES HIPKINS

Clare's last known letter. 'Mr. Jas. Hipkins' was a stranger who had written to the asylum asking how he was.

BIRDS NESTS

Clare's last poem, written a few months before he died.

Glossary

anker to hanker.
awe haw.
awthorn hawthorn.

baffles gaiters.
balk, baulk, bawk strip of grass dividing ploughed fields.
ball ox.
beatle hammer or mallet.
beavering hour break for refreshment.
bents stems of grass.
besprent sprinkled.
bill pruning-hook.
billet thick piece of firewood.
blea bleak or wild.
blealy bleakly or coldly.
blood walls wallflowers.
bottle bundle.
brake bracken.
brig bridge.
brustle to rustle.
bumbarrel long-tailed tit.

chelp to chirp.

chickering chirping.
chittering twittering.
chuff chubby.
cirging surging.
clack gossip.
clammed starved.
clamper to clump.
clippers sheep shearers.
closen small fields.
clown labourer.
clumpsing freezing.
coney rabbit.
copt (of hay) heaped up.
cot cottage.
cotter cottage-dweller.
crank croak.
creasing increasing.
crimpled wrinkled.
crizzle to crystallize.
croo to coo like a dove.
crumble crumb.
crumping crunching.

dimp to dimple.
dimute diminutive.
dither to shiver.
dizen to decorate.
dotterel pollard tree.
dowie dowdy.
drowking drooping.

edding heading, grass at end of ploughed field.
ekes increases.
elting damp.

firetail redstart.
flags rushes.

248

flirt to flutter.
fother to feed.
fotherer one who brings fodder.
frit frightened.

gad gadfly.
gen against.
glib or **glibbed** smooth or slippery.
goss gorse.
grain bough.
gris grist.

headach poppy.
heaves eaves.
hind farm servant.
hing to hang.
hirkle to crouch.
hirple to limp.
horse-blob marsh-marigold.
hugh huge.
hurd to hoard.
huzzing tumultuous.

jiliflower gillyflower, the clove-scented carnation.
jocolat chocolate.
joll to lurch.

knarled gnarled.

lare to rest.
larkheel larkspur.
lither lazy.

maul to drag along wearily.
max gin.
mayteys friends.
moilers labourers.
morts a large number.

mozzling mottled.
mulldering mouldering.

nap to nibble.
near never.
neatherd cowherd.
neuk nook.
nimble to move swiftly.

oddling solitary.
orison horizon.

pails a fence.
pattins overshoes.
pending depending.
pettichaps willow-warbler.
pill to peel.
pismire ant.
plash to splash.
platt flat bit of ground.
pleachy bleached.
poach porch.
pooty snail-shell.
popples poplars.
pranking flitting about.
prog or **proggle** to prod.
puddock kite.
pye magpie.

ramping romping.
rawky foggy.
runnel stream.

sallow willow.
sawn to saunter.
scrat to scratch.
scrip a shepherd's coat.

scrowed marked.
shoffle to shuffle.
sile to glide.
sinkfoil cinquefoil.
slive to slip.
sluther to slither.
snub stumpy.
soodle to dawdle.
sosh to swoop.
spindle stem.
spindling shooting.
sprent sprinkled.
sprotes small twigs.
squirking squeaking.
starnel starling.
sticker one who gathers sticks.
sticking stick-gathering.
stock cattle.
streck to stretch.
sturt to move suddenly.
suther to sigh, make a rushing noise, fly (of birds).
sutty sooty.
swaily shady.
swaliest shadiest.
swath or **swarth**   row of cut grass or corn.
swee to swing.
swee swaw seesaw.
swoof grief.
swop to swoop.

taw marble.
thack thatch.
thacker thatcher.
thrum to twang.
toze to snatch.
twitch couch grass.

waffling barking.

wain wagon.
watchet light blue.
waukly weakly.
wimmy full of whims.
witchens elms.

younker youngster.

zemblance resemblance.